SANTA ANA PUBLIC LIBRARY

GOD'S
LIBRARY

A Catholic Introduction
to the World's Greatest Book

Joe Paprocki

LOYOLAPRESS.

CHICAGO

LOYOLAPRESS.

3441 N. ASHLAND AVENUE
CHICAGO, ILLINOIS 60657
(800) 621-1008
WWW.LOYOLABOOKS.ORG

Nihil Obstat
Reverend John G. Lodge S.S.L., S.T.D.
Censor Deputatus
August 27, 2004

Imprimatur
Most Reverend Raymond E. Goedert, M.A., S.T.L., J.C.L.
Vicar General
Archdiocese of Chicago
August 31, 2004

The *Nihil Obstat* and *Imprimatur* are official declarations that a book is free of doctrinal and moral error. No implication is contained therein that those who have granted the *Nihil Obstat* and *Imprimatur* agree with the content, opinions, or statements expressed. Nor do they assume any legal responsibility associated with publication.

This volume is a substantial revision of *God's Library: Introducing Catholics to the Bible* published in 1999 by Twenty-Third Publications.

Cover image ©Volker Möhrke/CORBIS
Cover design by Michael Karter
Interior design by Arc Group Ltd

Library of Congress Cataloging-in-Publication Data
Paprocki, Joe.
  God's library : an introduction to the Bible / Joe Paprocki.
     p. cm.
  Includes bibliographical references.
  ISBN 0-8294-2069-X
  1. Bible—Introductions. I. Title.
BS445.P29 2005
220.6'1—dc22

2004014284

Printed in the United States of America
05 06 07 08 09 10 Bang 10 9 8 7 6 5 4 3 2 1

I dedicate this book to the late Sr. Georgine Smolinski, C.R., who firmly believed that a teenager could possibly be interested in the Bible, and to Fr. Terry Baum, S.J., for giving that teenager spiritual direction that has lasted a lifetime.

CONTENTS

ACKNOWLEDGMENTS

I would like to thank Pat Kahl for inviting me (a number of years ago) to do my first God's Library workshop with her wonderful sixth graders and catechists at St. Terrence in Alsip, Illinois. Thanks to Regina Bajko for speedy research, Andy Bocanegra for sharing his biblical knowledge over a cheeseburger, Steve Sutera for jogging my biblical memory over breakfast, and Joanne, Mike, and Amy for loving me so much I could bust.

Much thanks to Jim Manney and all the good folks at Loyola Press for giving *God's Library* a second life. Thanks to Rebecca Johnson for polishing the manuscript so thoroughly and effectively. Thanks to Jim Campbell and Tom McLaughlin for outstanding suggestions for improving upon the original manuscript. Thanks to Michael Cameron for his great work on the annotated bibliography for Catholic Scripture study.

Special thanks to the many Scripture professors at whose feet I was privileged to sit, especially: Mark Link, S.J.; Dr. Robert Ludwig; Dianne Bergant, C.S.A.; Donald Senior, C.P.; Barbara Reid, O.P.; Eugene LaVerdiere, S.S.S.; Leslie Hoppe, O.F.M.; Carroll Stuhlmueller, C.P.; and Carolyn Osiek, R.S.C.J.

ONE

Overcoming "Bibliaphobia"

In the famous cartoon *A Charlie Brown Christmas,* Charlie seeks the advice of his friend Lucy, explaining that he just doesn't feel right. Charlie listens as Lucy goes through a long list of phobias that might possibly explain Charlie's problem, including fears of responsibility, cats, staircases, the ocean, and crossing bridges. Finally, Lucy suggests that perhaps Charlie's problem is being caused by something called pantaphobia. When Lucy explains that pantaphobia is the fear of *everything,* Charlie shouts, "That's it!"

The truth is that most of us have some sort of fear. Hopefully, you do not suffer from pantaphobia, but many things about life can indeed be frightening. Two of the most common fears that people admit to are a fear of public speaking followed by a fear of death. Comedian Jerry Seinfeld points out how ironic it is that most of us have a greater fear of speaking at a funeral than we have of being the deceased person spoken of!

While surveys routinely reveal peoples' greatest fears, one fear often goes unnoticed. It is a fear that is common among Catholics. I call it *bibliaphobia,* or fear of the Bible (*biblia* = Bible; *phobia* = fear of). As Catholics, many of us were told that when it came to the idea of reading or studying the Bible, we should let Father explain it to us on Sunday. Even though Vatican II stressed the importance of becoming familiar with the Bible by reading and reflecting on the Scriptures on our own, it has been hard to shake the notion that Scripture study was something that Protestants did. As a result, many of us now feel at a loss when it comes to understanding—let alone explaining—the Bible to others. We fear the topic of the Bible coming up in conversation. We feel intimidated by many of our Protestant brothers and sisters who can quote chapter and verse. Most of all, we have no idea what to tell someone if they should ask, "Is it *true* that Noah built an ark or that Adam lived to be 930 years old or that Jonah was swallowed by a large fish?" What do we say? How do we answer such questions? What do we believe for ourselves?

"I Was Never Taught to Read the Bible . . ."

For many of us, the Bible was a very large book kept on a shelf in the living room or dining room and used mainly as a place to record the family history. It was less a book to read than a relic to store in the house, a sacramental that reminded us of the presence of God's word in the home. As children, many of us encountered the Bible only when we needed something heavy to flatten the wrinkles in a hastily glued school art project. Rare was the occasion that this great big book was pulled out to be read from. For one, it was too heavy. For another, it had words that sounded strange and foreign . . . too many "thee's" and "thou's" for our liking. More important, many of us were simply not encouraged to read the Bible. Some Catholics actually recall being discouraged from reading the Bible in the days before Vatican II.

Another reason Catholics shied away from the Bible was because we viewed the Bible as a Protestant thing. Suspicious of the axiom *Sola Scriptura!* (Scripture alone!) seen as a battle cry for Protestants, Catholics kept the Bible at arm's length, trusting the church hierarchy, the nuns, and our CCD teachers to sort out the Bible messages intended for our ears. As long as we had the sacraments, church Tradition, and Father's homily, we had little reason to sit down and read the Bible privately, let alone attempt to interpret the word of God.

The Underlying Causes of Bibliaphobia

Most phobias are an exaggerated or irrational fear, dread, or aversion to any object or stimulus. In most cases, there may indeed be something to fear, but the fear becomes disproportional or irrational. Bibliaphobia works in much the same way. While it is true that there are some things about the Bible that may be intimidating, many of us avoid it as though it were a swarm of bees. Let's take a look at some of the more intimidating aspects of the Bible that may be at the root of our bibliaphobia.

> *"It's too long!"* Most of us are accustomed to reading books that have legible print and are about 200–300 pages in length. The Bible, on the other hand, usually has very tiny print and contains anywhere between 1,000 and 2,500 pages, depending on which version we're reading.

"It has too many names I don't recognize." Eldad, Medad, Meshach, Shadrach, Abednego, Zephaniah, Zechariah, Caiaphas, Annas, etc. Who *are* these people? So-and-so begot so-and-so who begot so-and-so . . . These names don't ring any bells for us at first glance.

"It has too many places I've never heard of." Marah, Elim, Rephidim, Shiloh, Samaria, Colossae, Thessalonica . . . even the letter to the Philippians has nothing to do with the Philippines. Where *are* these places? It's hard to understand a story if we don't understand the setting.

"It uses images that don't belong to our time and culture." We live in an age of cell phones, the Internet, microwaves, CDs, DVDs, and HDTV. References to shekels, cubits, arks, nets, and mustard seeds often leave us scratching our heads.

"It's not like other books." Most books have a beginning, a middle, and an end and are divided up into chapters. The Bible has testaments, books, chapters, and verses. Most books are chronological. The Bible seems to jump around a lot.

"Some of the stories just seem incredible." Most of us have never seen burning bushes, or parting seas, or arks, or talking serpents, or people being swallowed by large fish. It's hard to understand these stories when we have no common frame of reference.

"You need to be a Scripture scholar to interpret the Bible." The Bible seems to be so complex and to contain so many layers of meaning that most of us feel inept and inadequate

when it comes to making biblical interpretations. Sometimes it feels as if you need to study a whole semester of graduate theology just to understand a few passages.

"I don't know anything about Judaism and that's all the Old Testament talks about." Most of us are struggling just to be good Christians. The Bible, on the other hand—especially the Old Testament (which is three-fourths of the entire Bible)—seems to require a great deal of knowledge about the Jewish faith and way of life.

"I honestly don't know if I can stomach some of it." Jesus talks about loving enemies, praying for persecutors, turning the other cheek, the blessings of being poor, and dying in order to live. How do we live these ideas today? Can we?

"I could never quote chapter and verse like many Protestants can!" On TV and in life, we see so many preachers, ministers, and ordinary people, most often Protestant, who can quote the Bible from memory, citing chapter and verse. Do we need to learn the Bible that way too? Many of us are not sure if we can or even want to.

Perhaps noting all of these common fears and concerns about the Bible has only confirmed your notion that the Bible is something to shy away from. On the contrary, I am just pointing out that these fears and concerns about the Bible are not yours alone. They are shared by many people, especially Catholics who have not had much Bible exposure and experience. But do not despair! Fear of the Bible can be overcome by tackling the above-mentioned fears and concerns with a commonsense understanding of the Bible, such as how it is put together and how we are to read and interpret it.

So how can you tell if you are suffering from bibliaphobia? Determine your level of bibliaphobic behavior by using the scale below to respond to each of the symptoms in this checklist.

0 = Totally Disagree
1 = Somewhat Disagree
2 = Somewhat Agree
3 = Totally Agree

_____ You have trouble locating even famous Bible stories and characters.

_____ You shy away from discussions about the Bible.

_____ You feel intimidated by those who you feel have more Bible knowledge.

_____ You have difficulty answering questions that children ask you about the Bible.

_____ You rarely attempt reading the Bible on your own.

_____ You feel inadequate when you consider attending Bible study.

_____ Locating a passage identified by book, chapter, and verse (e.g., 1 Pt 2:3) seems as difficult as solving an algebra problem.

_____ After reading a Bible passage, you often feel you have no idea what it meant.

_____ You find many Bible stories confusing.

_____ Your Bible is still in store-bought "mint" condition (give yourself an extra point if it is still encased in the store's shrink-wrap).

_____ **Write your total here.**

Now, match your score to one of these categories:
0 = None (You're perfectly at home with the Bible.)
1–10 = Mild (The Bible presents some challenges to you.)
11–20 = Moderate (You find the Bible to be most difficult.)
21–29 = Severe (You have a strong fear of the Bible.)
30–31 = Bibliaphobe Alert (You need immediate Bible
        therapy!)

Acknowledging the Problem

Our lack of knowledge about the Bible can often be an embarrassment. How can we, adult Catholic Christians, admit to not knowing or understanding the word of God? We may not even realize how inadequate our understanding of the Bible really is until we are put to the test.

Did someone say a test? What a great idea!

Take the B.A.T. (the Bible Awareness Test) to see just how familiar (or unfamiliar) you are with the Bible and its contents. Give yourself two minutes to find each of these stories or passages in the Bible. If you are able to find a story or passage in two minutes or fewer, place a checkmark next to it.

____ David and Goliath

____ Noah's ark

____ Jonah and the large fish

____ Moses crossing the Red Sea

____ Daniel in the lions' den

____ Zacchaeus the tax collector

____ Jesus walking on the water

_____ Pentecost

_____ Hg 2:1–3

_____ The second book of Chronicles, chapter 29, verses 9–15

Now, match the number of stories or passages you found to one of the categories below to determine your B.Q. (Bible Quotient).
10 = High (You probably don't need to read the rest of *God's Library*.)
7–9 = Average (Not bad, but keep reading.)
3–6 = Fair (*God's Library* is required reading.)
0–2 = Low (You *need God's Library*.)

This very unscientific test is only an indicator of how familiar or unfamiliar you are with the Bible. However, the reason we are not familiar with the Bible is because we often do not understand it, and as a result, we fear it. We always tend to fear those things with which we are most unfamiliar. We need to overcome our fears of the Bible by becoming more familiar with the Good Book. Don't let bibliaphobia get the best of you. Don't become an adult "Charlie Brown"–paralyzed by a fear that prevents you from living fully by discovering in the Bible what it truly means to live!

And Now, the Good News

The good news (aside from the gospel of Jesus Christ) is that, with a few tips and some practice, reading and understanding the Bible can become much easier and extremely fulfilling. The Bible was not written for scholars; it was written for you and me. The Bible is God speaking to you and me in the course of human events. It is meant to be read not only in churches and universities, but also in subways, at bus stops, in the cafeteria, in a rocking chair, in bed, or listened to on tape or CD as you drive. Sure, certain aspects of the Bible may seem intimidating, but when you stop to think about the fact that the Creator of the universe has something to say to *you,* it makes the notion of learning about the Bible a little bit more enticing!

The Bible has been a powerful influence in my own life and in the lives of countless numbers of people. Not only is it the story of people who lived thousands of years ago, but it is also the story of your life and my life. Every Bible story is a metaphor for the many experiences of God we all have had and will have in our lives. So as we prepare to look at burning bushes and parting seas, at the calming of storms, the healing of blind, deaf, and paralyzed people, and the raisings from the dead, know that somehow these experiences are part of our story.

Overcoming bibliaphobia is a matter of changing our perception of the Bible. The first thing we need to realize when considering the Good Book is that it isn't a book at all! The word *biblia* comes from the Greek, meaning "books." In reality, the Bible is a *collection* of books—seventy-three in all. For that reason, I prefer to think of the Bible as God's Library. What is a library other than books brought together in one place in order to give readers access to the entire collection? When we understand the Bible as God's Library, it changes our approach to how we are to read and understand its writings. We would never go to a library assuming that we are supposed to begin reading the first book on the first shelf and progress to the last book on the last shelf. Nor would we suppose that all of the books in a library are to be understood and read in exactly the same way or that all are the same type of literature. Once we learn how to use a library, we are capable of accessing the power of its contents. In the same way, once we learn how to use God's Library, the Bible, we will be able to access the mighty power of its contents.

So welcome to God's Library. Leave your bibliaphobia at the door and enter into a collection of writings about how God powerfully lives and moves in the lives of some very interesting people . . . including *you*.

QUESTIONS FOR REFLECTION AND DISCUSSION

- What was your experience of the Bible as a child . . . a teen . . . a young adult? What is your experience presently?

- What do you find most intimidating about the Bible?

- What do you find most attractive or inviting about the Bible?

- Who is someone you know who knows the Bible extremely well? Where did he or she get their knowledge of the Bible?

- How might a better understanding of the Bible make a difference in your life?

- What is the one thing you need to improve the most when it comes to knowing or understanding the Bible?

- How have you used libraries? Think about how libraries "work," and keep this description handy as you continue to read this book and become more familiar with God's Library, the Bible.

TWO

Welcome to God's Library!

O ver the years, countless people resolve, whether at New Year's or some other time, to read the Bible cover to cover. Perhaps you will as well. My guess is that your experience will go something like this. You begin with a great deal of enthusiasm, perhaps parceling out a special time each day to devote to reading the Bible. Genesis has enough interesting stories to keep you going but gives rather too much practical advice on ark building. Exodus is full of drama, with the ten plagues and the Red Sea, and rebuilds the enthusiasm that began to flag in the genealogy sections of Genesis. Leviticus is often the deal breaker. Laws, rules, directions, penalties . . . ugh. And if you somehow manage to make it through Leviticus, Numbers is almost guaranteed to finish you off. You give up on your reading project, concluding that the Bible is a book written for scholars and not for ordinary folk like us.

Why do I make this dire prediction? Simply because reading the Bible from cover to cover is a flawed approach that treats the Bible like an ordinary book. Even such humongous tomes as *War and Peace* can be conquered using this basic head-down, barrel-through method of reading cover to cover. However, the Bible is no ordinary book. It is a collection of books, a library. Sure, the Bible *can* be read from cover to cover, and many have done so with great delight. However, many others have tried and failed, only to miss out on the powerful message of God's word. We need to approach the Bible as if we were climbing the steps to enter a library building. Like any library, the Bible makes available to us a rich variety of readings from which we may choose selections according to our needs. Consider the Bible a library that you will become more familiar with over time. The more familiar you become with God's Library, the more you will use it. The more you use it, the more of it you will read and understand. The more of it you read and understand, the closer you will be to the God who speaks to you in and through it!

How a Library Works

Let's flesh out this comparison between the Bible and a library by thinking about how we "use" our local libraries and how we might "use" the Bible. Over the course of our lives, most of us have made numerous trips to libraries in our schools and communities. We go for various reasons: research, enrichment, entertainment, to find peace and quiet, etc. But once we're there, how do we use a library? It's easy. For most of us, it entails the following:

- check the computerized card catalogue for the location of a particular author or book title or subject matter, or ask a librarian to point out the location of a particular type of literature

- locate the section of the library in which that type of literature (or in which the book's assigned number) can be found

- locate the item(s) you are interested in reading

- check out the item(s)

- take the item(s) home and read at your leisure or as needed

Libraries are familiar, often comforting, places. Unless you were shushed one too many times as a child, you probably don't associate anxiety with visiting the library. So with that in mind, let's visit God's Library. We come to God's Library for many reasons: research, prayer, inspiration, curiosity, enjoyment, encouragement, etc. We also come to it with different tastes. Some of us prefer the psalms and the proverbs to the letters and the parables. What we find when we enter God's Library is an arrangement not unlike the library we just visited. In fact, we find the following:

- a "card catalogue"—the table of contents

- two large "halls" or "wings"—the Old and New Testaments

- smaller sections or "stack rooms" within these two great halls: Pentateuch (or Torah), History, Wisdom, Prophets, Gospels, Acts, Letters, and Revelation

In fact, if the Bible were truly a library building, its floor plan would look something like this.

Let's take a closer look now at the various parts of God's Library.

Using the Catalogue

Nowadays, most library card catalogues are computerized. However, the basic idea has not changed. You can still locate a book using the author's name or the book's title, or you can use a keyword search to find books on a particular subject. Many of us when looking for a particular book are guilty of ignoring the catalogue at the library and heading straight for the shelves. More often than not, we end up searching aisle after aisle and shelf after shelf with little or no luck. In much the same way, many of us attempt to locate particular Scripture passages in the Bible without using the "catalogue," or the table of contents. If we know the book, chapter, and verses that we are looking for, the Bible's table of contents will help us. Later, we'll learn how to find a Bible passage when we don't know its book, chapter, or verse. In a Bible's table of contents, you will more than likely find the following:

- a list of the books of the Bible in the order in which they appear in the Old and New Testaments as well as the page on which each book begins

- an alphabetical listing of the books

- an alphabetical listing of the abbreviation of each book

A table of contents in a typical Bible will look something like this.

Old Testament

Book	Abbreviation	Page
Genesis	Gn	1
Exodus	Ex	50
Leviticus	Lv	100
Numbers	Nm	130
Deuteronomy	Dt	170

. . . and so on, listing all forty-six Old Testament books. In the same way, the New Testament listing would look like this.

New Testament

Book	Abbreviation	Page
Matthew	Mt	1000
Mark	Mk	1050
Luke	Lk	1075
John	Jn	1115

. . . and so on, listing all twenty-seven New Testament books. (Some Bibles start over at page 1 for the New Testament.) For a complete list of all of the books of the Bible and their abbreviations, see the appendix to this book, page 119 (or pick up a Bible and check it out for yourself).

Sometimes a table of contents will include a separate alphabetical listing of the books in the Old and New Testaments. It might look something like this.

Old Testament

Book	Abbreviation	Page
Amos	Am	900
Baruch	Bar	875
1 Chronicles	1 Chr	350
2 Chronicles	2 Chr	400
Daniel	Dn	950

. . . and so on.

New Testament

Book	Abbreviation	Page
Acts of the Apostles	Acts	1200
Colossians	Col	1300
1 Corinthians	1 Cor	1250
2 Corinthians	2 Cor	1275
Ephesians	Eph	1290

. . . and so on.

Now that we see how the Bible's catalogue is arranged, let's take a closer look at how to use it..

Is It "Judg.," "Jg," or "Jgs"?

Learning to use the abbreviation page of your Bible is critical to being able to locate Bible passages. One thing to consider, however, is that not all Bibles abbreviate books in the same way. A little later on, we'll discuss the differences between various Bibles and how to choose one, but for now, just know that different Bibles abbreviate the names of books in different ways. For example, the book of Judges can be found abbreviated as Judg., Jg, or Jgs, depending on which Bible translation you are looking at. Knowing that Bibles abbreviate books differently will help avoid a great deal of confusion, especially if you are in a group of people using a variety of Bible translations or editions.

THE BIBLE'S BOOK NUMBERING SYSTEM

In any library, you need to understand the numbering system used to shelve the books in a particular order so that you can find what you need. The same is true of locating passages in God's Library. No, the Bible does not use the Dewey decimal system or the Library of Congress classification system, but instead has its own system of identifying books, chapters, and verses. It's called Scripture citation. You've seen it before. It looks like this.

1 Pt 2:1–4

And like any system of classification, it will look like a foreign language until you learn the rules. The key to understanding Scripture citation is really quite simple. No matter the Bible translation or edition you are using, citations always follow this format: the name of the book, followed by the chapter number, followed by the verse number (or the begininng and ending verse numbers). The chapter number and the verse number(s) are separated by a colon. So,

1 Pt 2:1–4

means

> 1 Pt (name of the book) 2 (chapter number):1–4 (verses
> 1 through 4)

But what's a 1 Pt? If you refer to the abbreviation section in the alphabetical listing of books in your Bible's table of contents, you'll discover that 1 Pt is the first letter of Peter. So the citation refers to the first letter of Peter, chapter 2, verses 1 through 4.

Here are a few more examples.

> Jgs 15:6–15 = the book of Judges, chapter fifteen, verses six through fifteen

> Zep 3:18–19 = the book of Zephaniah, chapter three, verses eighteen through nineteen

> Jn 7:3–6, 10 = the Gospel of John, chapter seven, verses three through six and verse ten

> Ti 2:11–14 = the letter to Titus, chapter two, verses eleven through fourteen

Now, practice with the following Scripture citations. If you need help with the abbreviations, use your Bible's table of contents or see page 119 of this book. The answers can be found on page 34.

Quiz 1

1. Is 42:5–10 _____

2. Hg 3:6–11 _____

3. 1 Mc 6:1–6 _____

4. 3 Jn 1:2–4 _____

5. Jas 2:7–9 _____

6. Mk 9:8–15 _____

Now, try the same thing but in reverse order: take the following passages described in prose and write them in citation form. The first one has been done as an example. The answers can be found on page 34.

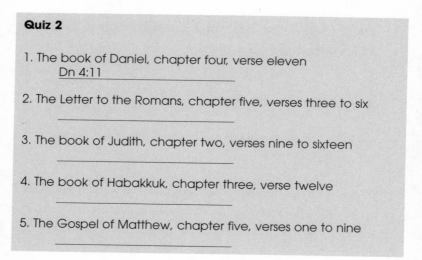

Quiz 2

1. The book of Daniel, chapter four, verse eleven
   Dn 4:11 _____

2. The Letter to the Romans, chapter five, verses three to six
   _____

3. The book of Judith, chapter two, verses nine to sixteen
   _____

4. The book of Habakkuk, chapter three, verse twelve
   _____

5. The Gospel of Matthew, chapter five, verses one to nine
   _____

Now that you know how to locate passages by book, chapter, and verse, let's turn to how you can locate a particular story in the Bible when you have no idea what book it is in.

Bookmarks and Training Wheels

Think back to when you learned how to ride a two-wheeler. More than likely, you used training wheels until you developed your own sense of balance. After much practice, the training wheels came off and you were on your way. In the same way, we are going to look at a simple tool that can be used like training wheels until you develop your own sense of how to maneuver through the Bible.

What should you do when you want to find the story of David and Goliath but you don't know what book it is in? How does one develop a familiarity with the Bible so that wonderful stories and famous characters can be quickly located? In the back of this book you will find eight bookmarks (pg. 123). You may cut these out or copy the text onto heavy stock for sturdier bookmarks.

Recall that earlier we discussed how the Bible is split into two main parts, the Old and New Testaments. These testaments are then commonly divided again into four more parts. These divisions are listed in the table below.

Old Testament	New Testament
Pentateuch (Torah)	Gospels
History	Acts
Wisdom	Letters
Prophets	Revelation

Now that we know the names, let's do a little exercise. Using your Bible's table of contents, locate the last page of the book of Malachi (which is the last page of the Old Testament) and the first page of the Gospel of Matthew (which is the first page of the New Testament). Now, take a look at how the Bible is separated. Observe how large the Old Testament is compared to the New Testament. Keep in mind the clearest and simplest distinction between the Old and New Testaments:

The Old Testament is the story of the people of Israel *before* the birth of Jesus Christ.

The New Testament is the story of the *Christian* experience, beginning with the life of Jesus Christ and continuing with the early church.

Once you have this clear distinction in your head, you will have a better understanding of where to begin searching for stories in the Bible by asking yourself one simple question: Is this story directly related to the life of Jesus and the early church? If the answer is yes, then you'll be looking in the New Testament. If not, you'll be searching through the Old Testament.

"Great," you may be saying, "but I still have to sift through a thousand pages to find the story I'm looking for!" This is true, but what we are about to do is to break the Bible down into the smaller sections mentioned in the table. The following outlines, which are also found on the bookmarks, can be seen as a brief introduction to the highlights of each section of the Bible. By using the bookmarks and the highlights outline, you can have easy access to the various parts of the Bible.

HIGHLIGHTS OF THE OLD TESTAMENT

Find the four bookmarks for the Old Testament that you cut out of the back of this book (see page 123) or that you copied onto another sheet of paper. Lay them out side-by-side next to your Bible.

Pentateuch: The first five books of the Old Testament, Genesis through Deuteronomy

Place the Pentateuch (pronounced Pen-tuh-tuke) bookmark on the last page of the book of Deuteronomy. The pages from the beginning of Genesis to this bookmark make up the section called the Pentateuch (Torah in the Hebrew Scriptures), meaning the five books of the Law. This section captures the beginnings of the relationship between God and the people of Israel with the central focus being the Exodus event . . . the experience of being led from slavery to freedom. Here are some of the highlights of this section:

- the creation stories

- Adam and Eve

- Cain and Abel

- Noah's ark

- the tower of Babel

- Sodom and Gomorrah

- Abraham and Sarah

- Isaac and Rebekah

- Jacob and Esau

- Joseph (the coat of many colors)

- Moses (in the reeds, the burning bush, the ten plagues, the crossing of the Red Sea, the Passover, the Ten Commandments, the Ark of the Covenant, the journey through the desert, the death of Moses)

- the twelve tribes of Israel

- the laws, traditions, and feasts of Israel

History: Joshua through 2 Maccabees

Place the bookmark labeled History on the last page of 2 Maccabees. The section from the Pentateuch bookmark to this bookmark makes up the History section of God's Library. This section records the story of the people of Israel who, under various leaders (judges and kings), fought to establish and keep the Promised Land. Here are the highlights of this section:

- Joshua (crossing the Jordan, the walls of Jericho)

- Samson and Delilah

- Ruth and Naomi

- Samuel (request for a king)

- King Saul

- David and Goliath; King David

- Solomon (the temple, queen of Sheba)

- Elijah and Elisha

- many kings, battles, and genealogies

- division of the kingdom

- exile and return

- Judith and Esther

Wisdom: Job through Sirach

Place the bookmark labeled Wisdom at the end of the book of Sirach (or Ecclesiasticus, as it is called in some Bibles). You're now ready to explore the Wisdom section of the Bible, which includes everything from the History bookmark to this bookmark. While the Bible is full of wisdom, this particular section gathers together all the wisdom teachings of the people of Israel that were collected over thousands of years of wandering the desert, living in the Promised Land, worshipping in the temple, and struggling through exile. This section includes many anecdotes, sayings, prayers, poems, and songs. Here are some highlights:

- Job's suffering

- 150 Psalms for all occasions*

- hundreds of proverbs

- wise sayings, including "Vanity of vanities, all things are vanity!" and "There is a time for everything" and "A faithful friend is a sturdy shelter"

- a romantic love song (Song of Songs, or Song of Solomon)

- thousands more sayings about wisdom, prudence, good health, wealth, holiness, family, friends, misery, death, and even table etiquette

* While the Psalms are not technically considered wisdom literature (they are more appropriately liturgical hymns), Psalms traditionally have been placed with the Wisdom books.

Prophets: Isaiah through Malachi

Place the last of your four Old Testament bookmarks, labeled Prophets, at the end of the book of Malachi, which is also the last page of the Old Testament. Welcome to the last section of the Old Testament—the Prophets (everything from your Wisdom bookmark to this one). The prophets were not concerned with foretelling the future. Their purpose was to call the people of Israel to return to their past fidelity to God lest they face dire consequences. And when the people of Israel found themselves doomed in exile, the prophets held out hope for the future. This hope was the promise of a messiah and an everlasting kingdom. Yet even these assurances of a future are accompanied by a call for a return to the fidelity of the past. Here are some highlights:

- The major (meaning lengthier) prophets
    - Isaiah (Immanuel, "the people who walked in darkness have seen a great light," "comfort my people," etc.)
    - Jeremiah (call of Jeremiah, exile and return)
    - Ezekiel (the dry bones)

- The minor (meaning briefer) prophets, including
    - Daniel (the lions' den, Shadrach, Meshach, and Abednego)
    - Hosea (the unfaithful wife)
    - Joel (the Day of the Lord)
    - Amos (the call to justice)
    - Jonah (swallowed by a large fish)

HIGHLIGHTS OF THE NEW TESTAMENT

Find the four bookmarks for the New Testament that you cut out of the back of this book (see page 125) or that you copied onto another sheet of paper. Lay them out side-by-side next to your Bible.

Gospels: Matthew, Mark, Luke, and John

Place the bookmark labeled Gospels at the end of the Gospel of John. Between the bookmark for the Prophets and this bookmark is the beginning of the New Testament. It is also the section of God's Library in which we walk with Jesus. The Gospels (Matthew, Mark, Luke, and John) contain the stories that are most sacred to our Christian faith and heritage: stories of the life, teachings, miracles, passion, death, and resurrection of Jesus of Nazareth. If you're looking for a story about Jesus, this is the place to look. Here are some highlights:

- the birth of Jesus (the Magi, the shepherds, etc.)

- the Holy Family (Mary and Joseph)

- the finding of Jesus in the temple

- the temptation in the desert and the baptism of Jesus

- the Beatitudes and the Our Father

- parables (the prodigal son, the good samaritan, the sower, the mustard seed, etc.)

- the Golden Rule and the great commandment

- numerous miracles (calming of the storm, raising of Lazarus, changing water into wine, feeding of the 5,000, walking on water, healing of the blind, deaf, and paralyzed, etc.)

- the Last Supper, Eucharist, and the washing of the feet

- the agony in the garden

- Peter's denial and Judas's betrayal

- the way of the cross

- the Crucifixion

- the Resurrection and appearances

- dozens of fascinating characters: Zacchaeus, Pontius Pilate, Mary Magdalene, Nicodemus, the Samaritan woman, Martha and Mary, etc.

- powerful images such as the Bread of Life, the Light of the World, the Way, the Truth, and the Life

Acts of the Apostles

Finding this section of the Bible is easy because it is just one book: the Acts of the Apostles. Place the bookmark labeled Acts of the Apostles at the end of this book and relive the experience of the early Christian community. In many ways, the book of Acts is a sequel to the Gospel of Luke because Luke and Acts were written by the same author. Here are some highlights of the Acts:

- Jesus' ascension

- the descent of the Holy Spirit on Pentecost

- descriptions of the communal life of the early church

- Stephen's martyrdom

- Philip and the Ethiopian

- Saul's conversion and baptism

- the missionary work of Peter, Saul (Paul), Barnabas, and others

- miracles performed through Peter and Paul

- Paul's travels, imprisonment, trials, shipwreck, and arrival in Rome

Letters (also called Epistles): Romans through Jude

Place the bookmark labeled Letters at the end of the letter of Jude. Everything from the Acts of the Apostles bookmark up to this one represents the communications of the early church, before e-mail, phones, and faxes. A little more than half of the twenty-one letters, or epistles, are attributed to Paul and the Pauline tradition. All of the letters are addressed to communities of Christians and to the leaders of these communities and were designed to teach, admonish, encourage, correct, and update the various churches. Here are some highlights:

- The letters of Paul (such as Romans, 1 and 2 Corinthians, Galatians, and Ephesians) feature theology, teachings, and exhortations concerning
    - grace
    - justification by faith
    - the Law
    - the Eucharist
    - the metaphor of the Body
    - variety and unity of gifts
    - ministry
    - suffering
    - Christ and his cross
    - Christian conduct

- James (faith and good works and anointing of the sick)

- 1 Peter (be prepared to explain your hope)

- 1 John ("Beloved, let us love one another . . .")

Revelation

Place the last bookmark, labeled Revelation, at the end of the book of Revelation and you've reached the end of the Bible. As you enter the book of Revelation, be aware that it is one of the most misunderstood books of the Bible. Many falsely use this book to predict the end of the world. Written in apocalyptic language, the book of Revelation uses many symbols and figurative language to describe the eternal struggle between good and evil. Despite all of the frightening imagery, the uplifting conclusion of this book is that good has and will always prevail. Here are the highlights:

- visions and messages to the seven churches

- the scroll and the Lamb

- the 144,000 saved

- the seven trumpets

- the woman and the dragon

- the King of kings

- the thousand-year reign

- the new heaven and new earth

- the new Jerusalem

- "Come, Lord Jesus!"

Practicing with Your "Training Wheels"

Now that your bookmarks are in place, practice locating some of the highlights outlined on the bookmarks themselves or on the previous few pages. Browse through a section of God's Library and search for some of the famous characters and place-names. Don't set out to read whole sections. For now, just browse around until you discover passages that you are particularly interested in reading right now. If you don't understand a section or the reading is becoming tedious and difficult to understand, move on.

As you become more and more skilled at Bible reading, you can return to the more difficult and challenging sections. As you tackle these more difficult sections, you may wish to consult books about the Bible that can help you make sense of what you are reading. (See page 111 for a list of suggested readings.) For now, focus on getting to know the sections of the Bible so that you've got a firm sense of what can be found in each section. Most important, use your bookmarks to become more familiar with where these various sections of the Bible are. Your bookmarks will act as training wheels for the time being, assisting you in traversing the terrain of the Bible. Eventually, however, the training wheels must come off. When you feel you have worked hard at getting to know the locations of the various sections of the Bible, remove your bookmarks and continue trying to locate passages, stories, and characters in their respective sections. You should find that by familiarizing yourself with the themes and topics treated in various sections, you are able to find particular stories and passages more quickly and with greater confidence. Develop your God's Library skills by doing the following exercise.

Quiz 3

Read the list of stories and characters below and match the letter of the section of the Bible that you believe includes this story or character. See page 34 for the answers.

a. Pentateuch b. History   c. Wisdom   d. Prophets
e. Gospels   f. Acts   g. Letters   h. Revelation

____ 1. Solomon's temple

____ 2. The Seventh Trumpet

____ 3. Jonah and the large fish

____ 4. Saul's conversion

____ 5. Noah's ark

____ 6. Jacob and Esau

____ 7. The scriptural way of the cross

____ 8. Stephen's martyrdom

____ 9. Paul writing to the people of Ephesus

____ 10. The New Jerusalem

____ 11. David and Goliath

____ 12. Moses and the burning bush

____ 13. Zacchaeus

____ 14. The raising of Lazarus

____ 15. The dry bones

____ 16. Joseph, the "coat of many colors"

____ 17. Justification by faith

____ 18. The Holy Spirit on Pentecost

____ 19. Samson and Delilah

____ 20. The Ten Commandments

QUESTIONS FOR REFLECTION AND DISCUSSION

• Which Bible stories are the most difficult for you to find?

• Did you ever try to read the Bible cover to cover? What was your experience?

- In what ways can the table of contents pages of your Bible assist you in your prayer life? In your Bible study?

- What are the eight sections of God's Library? Can you briefly summarize what and who can be found in each (without peeking at the bookmarks)?

- How can breaking the Bible down into these eight sections help you in your knowledge of and familiarity with the Bible?

- As you practiced with your bookmarks, which section of the Bible did you discover for the first time?

- What section of the Bible do you look forward to getting to know better? Why?

Answer Key

Quiz 1: 1. Isaiah chapter forty-two, verses five to ten; 2. Haggai chapter three, verses six to eleven; 3. First book of Maccabees chapter six, verses one to six; 4. Third letter of John chapter one, verses two to four; 5. Letter of James chapter two, verses seven to nine; 6. The Gospel of Mark chapter nine, verses eight to fifteen.

Quiz 2: 1. Dn 4:11; 2. Rom 5:3–6; 3. Jdt 2:9–16; 4. Hb 3:12; 5. Mt 5:1–9.

Quiz 3: 1. b; 2. h; 3. d; 4. f; 5. a; 6. a; 7. e; 8. f; 9. g; 10. h; 11. b; 12. a; 13. e; 14. e; 15. d; 16. a; 17. g; 18. f; 19. b; 20. a.

THREE

The Bible as a Time
Capsule

Some years ago, Pepsi ran a television commercial that took place in a futuristic setting with a professor leading a group of students on an archeological dig. As they all drink from their Pepsi cans, one of them unearths a find—an object caked over with centuries of mud and dirt. Unable to make out what the object is, the professor places it in a device that quickly removes all of the layers of dirt only to reveal an empty bottle of Coca-Cola. With puzzled expressions, all of the students look at the object and ask the professor, "What is it?" The professor, with the same puzzled expression tilts the bottle this way and that before responding, "I have no idea!"

What this clever commercial attempted to show us, apart from the imagined future ascendancy of Pepsi products, is how something that once was a familiar sight and a household name can fade from memory and become so anachronistic that no one can identify it or make sense out of it. For our purposes, the point is well taken and can be applied to our exploration of God's Library. Much of the Bible, written centuries ago, is as foreign to many of us as that Coca-Cola bottle appeared to be to those students in the commercial. Characters, places, phrases, stories, and words that were easily identified and understood by the people of biblical times can be frustratingly strange to people of the twenty-first century. Quite often, when we read a segment of God's Library, we react the same way the students in the commercial reacted, by asking, "What is it? What does it mean?"

Becoming more familiar with the structure of God's Library was the first step in overcoming bibliaphobia. Now, we have to face up to the daunting task of trying to understand what it is that we are reading. For many of us, once we actually find the Scripture passage, our joy is short-lived because we realize that we are dealing with material that was written long ago in a land far away from our front door. We get frustrated when we realize that we have little or no idea of what we just read or how to properly understand it. We need some assistance in accessing and unleashing the power of God's word. For many of us, this word may seem buried under centuries of dirt, clay, and dried mud, preventing us from applying it to our present-day experience.

So far, our primary metaphor for the Bible has been that of a library. Another helpful way to think about the Bible is as a time capsule.

We all know what a time capsule is and how it works. People gather objects that convey the mood of their time—the fads, the defining moments, the customs, the famous people, the music, the headlines, the milestones, the accomplishments, and so on. These objects are placed in a container that is sealed and buried or placed somewhere with the idea that it will not be unearthed or opened until a much later date by people of another time, another era, another experience. The hope is that when people of some future era uncover the time capsule and examine the objects placed within, the experience of the past will come alive for them. By examining these objects from the past and seeking explanations for items that are foreign and mysterious, the people who unearthed the time capsule will make a connection with the people who buried it years before. The Bible attempts to do the very same thing for us. Not only is the Bible God's Library, it is also a time capsule from the people of Israel and the early church.

My, How Things Have Changed!

Change used to occur very slowly in our world—until the Industrial Revolution, that is. Cultures and societies that remained virtually unchanged for centuries suddenly faced an explosion of inventions that changed the face of the world forever. Today, change is occurring at such a rapid rate that it is quite reasonable to assume that something that was brand-new only a few years ago is now completely obsolete. No doubt, the computer on which I wrote this book is by now considered a dinosaur.

Think of all of the things that just a few short years ago were familiar household items but that today are completely foreign to many young people. For example,

- record players

- Beta VCRs

- eight-track tapes

- mimeograph machines

- filmstrips

- phones with dials

- flashcubes

- dot matrix printers

- typewriters

- slide rules

- 8-mm movie film

The list could go on. The point is, in just a few short years, things can change so much that we can lose any knowledge or understanding of how things used to work.

Now, think of the Bible. We're no longer talking about a few short years or decades or even a few centuries. Much of the Bible was written more than two thousand years ago. If you think things have changed a great deal over the past few years, imagine how much has changed over the last two or three thousand years. Not to mention the fact that the Bible comes to us from a land several thousand miles away from where most of us live and was written in a language quite different from the one spoken in your home or around the water coolers in your office. It is no wonder that some of the following things found in the Bible are as strange to us as an eight-track tape or a mimeograph machine might seem to our young people:

ephah	cubit	manna
shekel	myrrh	lyre
diadem	drachma	dromedary
scroll	mammon	sackcloth

Those are just things. What about formerly well-known people and places?

Sadducees	Ephesus	Esau
Capernaum	Meribah	Pharisees
Zealots	Jairus	Lake Gennesaret
Boaz	Nicodemus	Sanhedrin

It's no wonder that we sometimes get a little frustrated when we read the Bible and come across some of these words that may mean absolutely *nothing* to us. It is as though we are looking through someone else's photo album without them nearby to explain what and who we are looking at. Without some assistance, we will find ourselves scratching our heads and perhaps giving up. Fortunately, help is right at our fingertips. The Bible may seem to us like a time capsule that is difficult to understand in our contemporary times, but the secrets of the past can be revealed to us by reading the tiny print at the bottom of each Bible page. Prepare to enter the world of footnotes, cross-references, concordances, and commentaries. Before we do that, however, try testing your biblical knowledge of some of the items mentioned in the previous lists.

Multiple Choice Quiz

Test your knowledge of these biblical people, places, and things. Answers are on page 52.

_____ 1. An *ephah* is: (a) a type of rough adobe house lived in by Ephesians; (b) a unit of measure equal to one yard; (c) a dry measure equal to half a bushel; (d) the headscarf worn by unmarried Jewish women

_____ 2. *Manna* is: (a) the Hebrew word for man; (b) the substance the Israelites ate in the desert; (c) the town where Zacchaeus lived; (d) money or material things

_____ 3. A *drachma* is: (a) another name for a camel; (b) an ancient Greek silver coin; (c) one of the main items of property a bride brings to a marriage; (d) a turbanlike crown

_____ 4. A *lyre* is: (a) a stringed instrument similar to a harp; (b) a wineskin made from the stomach of a goat; (c) a form of Roman currency; (d) a wind instrument similar to a flute

_____ 5. A *scroll* is: (a) the name given to a Jewish priest; (b) Greek for "synagogue"; (c) a unit of measure equal to a foot; (d) a book formed out of rolled-up papyrus

_____ 6. *Esau* refers to: (a) the village where Jesus raised Lazarus from the dead; (b) the name of a temple official; (c) the name of Jacob's brother; (d) the name of one of the twelve apostles

_____ 7. *Jairus* was the name of: (a) the man whose daughter Jesus raised from the dead; (b) the tax collector Jesus called down from the tree; (c) the town toward which the two disciples walked when Jesus appeared to them; (d) Moses's father-in-law

_____ 8. The *Sadducees* were: (a) a fourth-century BC Egyptian dynasty; (b) people who were very sad, you see?; (c) a separatist sect living in the desert; (d) a priestly aristocracy from which came the high priest

_____ 9. *Nicodemus* was: (a) a member of the Sanhedrin who came to Jesus at night; (b) one of the criminals crucified next to Jesus; (c) the high priest who sent Jesus to Pilate; (d) the name of the first gentile converted by Paul

_____10. *Ephesus* was the name of: (a) the town whose walls fell down at the trumpet's blast; (b) one of the twelve apostles, Peter, in Greek; (c) the city to which Paul addressed his letter to the Ephesians; (d) one of the twelve tribes of Israel

Footnotes, Cross-References, Concordances, and Commentaries to the Rescue

Here's a Bible passage from the book of Deuteronomy concerning a law of marriage, which at first glance may seem difficult to understand. Read it over and see how much of it makes sense to you.

5 When brothers live together and one of them dies without a son, the widow of the deceased shall not marry anyone outside the family; but her husband's brother shall go to her and perform the duty of a brother-in-law by marrying her. 6 The first-born son she bears shall continue the line of the deceased brother, that his name may not be blotted out from Israel. 7 If, however, a man does not care to marry his brother's wife, she shall go up to the elders at the gate and declare, "My brother-in-law does not intend to perform his duty toward me and refuses to perpetuate his brother's name in Israel." 8 Thereupon, the elders of his city shall summon him and admonish him. If he persists in saying, "I am not willing to marry her," 9* his sister-in-law, in the presence of the elders, shall go up to him and strip his sandal from his foot and spit in his face, saying publicly, "This is how one should be treated who will not build up his brother's

family!" 10 And his lineage shall be spoken of in Israel as "the family of the man stripped of his sandal." (Dt 25:5–10)

The idea of spitting in someone's face is easily understood and even today would be seen as a humiliating gesture. But, what's all this about stripping a man of his sandal? It seems far worse to have someone spit in your face than to take away a shoe. Yet, this passage tells us that the people of Israel will remember the ne'er-do-well brother-in-law, *not* as the one who had his face spat upon, but as the "man *stripped of his sandal*." What's going on here? How do we understand this passage? What does it mean to us today? Where do we go for help?

The answer may lie in your Bible at the bottom of the page on which this passage is located (depending on which version of the Bible you're using). You'll notice that in this translation, verse 9 has an asterisk next to the verse number. This symbol indicates that there is additional information about this verse in a footnote. (Be aware that while different Bibles use different symbols to indicate a footnote, the most common symbols are an asterisk or consecutive letters of the alphabet.) So what's with the sandal? Here's the footnote for verse 9 in the New American Bible.

25:9 The penalty decreed for a man who refuses to comply with this law of family loyalty is public disgrace (the widow is to spit in his face) and the curse of poverty; sandals were proverbially a man's cheapest possession (cf Am 2, 6; 8, 6), and therefore "a man without sandals" was the poorest of the poor.

Aha. Now, we are getting somewhere. Here's an example of a phrase that meant one thing to certain people a few thousand years ago but holds little meaning for us today. Yet, when we read the footnote provided in God's Library, we see clearly how this act of removing a man's sandal was understood as a symbol of disgrace and a curse. Further, this footnote gives a cross-reference to the book of Amos. The abbreviation *cf* (short for confer, Latin for "compare") in the footnote indicates another passage that we should look up. If we find Amos 2:6, we discover the following quote: "Thus says the LORD: / For three crimes of Israel, and for four, / I will not revoke my word; / Because they sell the just man for silver, / and the poor man for a pair of sandals." Likewise, in Amos 8:6 we find this: "We will buy the lowly man for silver, / and the poor man for a pair of sandals."

The footnote and the cross-references provide readers with a clearer understanding of why this action of stripping a man of his sandal would be seen as such a powerful gesture. With this knowledge, we can go back to the original passage and reread it with a fuller understanding of what it meant to the people of Israel and of the role that the Law had in their lives.

Reading footnotes and cross-references may seem like a lot of work, but it is well worth it if we remember that we are reading the story of *our* salvation history. There are other payoffs as well. Once you look up a footnote or a cross-reference, you come away with an understanding that deepens your overall comprehension of the Bible because chances are, if you bump into a confusing word or phrase in one passage, it will come up in another. For example, take a look at the following passage that you've probably read numerous times: "Now the people were filled with expectation, and all were asking in their hearts whether John might be the Messiah. John answered them all, saying, 'I am baptizing you with water, but one mightier than I is coming. I am not worthy to loosen the thongs of his sandals'" (Lk 3:15–16). Now that our research has revealed that a man's sandal was his cheapest possession, we see how profound John the Baptist's statement is: he declares himself unworthy to touch Jesus' cheapest possession, namely, his sandal. By the way, we've also discovered a response to the age-old complaint of many Christians who feel that reading the Old Testament is a waste of time, thinking that it has nothing to teach us about Jesus. Think again. The Old Testament understanding of a man's sandal as his cheapest possession sheds light on this New Testament passage concerning John the Baptist's perspective on Jesus.

Footnotes provide us with many different types of information. Here are some examples.

- the meaning(s) of a word or phrase

- the historical setting of a story

- geographical locations

- important dates

- how certain stories and people are related

- references to other languages and an explanation of nuances in the original language that may be lost in the translation to English

- theological insight

- patterns to watch for

- customs and traditions of biblical peoples

- cross-references to similar occurrences of the same word, phrase, person, or situation

Footnotes provide a tool for scraping away centuries of "dirt and mud" to discover the true meaning of the word of God. By using footnotes, you will be able to see many passages in the Bible in a whole new light. Footnotes didn't just appear in the Bible. We can thank Scripture scholars and archeologists who have literally dug and scraped until they painstakingly uncovered insights into the past that allow us to bring the word of God to the present and carry it into the future. (For that reason, it's important to have a Bible that incorporates the best of Catholic Scripture scholarship. But we'll talk more about selecting a Bible later.) Now, let's practice looking up some footnotes.

Read the following Scripture stories along with any footnotes that are provided with the text. Make a brief list of any new information you learn.

- Noah's ark (Gn 6:5–22)

- the covenant with Abram (Gn 15)

- the call of Moses (Ex 3:4–22)

- Psalm 22

- the genealogy of Jesus and the birth of Jesus (Mt 1)

- the vocation of Saul (Acts 9:1–30)

- the woman and the dragon (Rv 12)

Learning to Cross-Reference

Footnotes may seem confusing at first glance until we learn how to find the information tied to these little symbols. In the same way, cross-references may look extremely off-putting. We may find a section of text near the bottom of our Bible page that contains an extensive list of numbers or letters and Bible passages. Here's an example of what it may look like in your Bible.

a Prv 8:14f. *b* Prv 1:6; Sir 39:1ff; 42:19f; Dn 2:21. *c* 1Kgs 3:28; Jb 29:8ff, 21f. *d* Sir 15:6; 41:12f; Is 56:5.

What's all this, then? Once again, you need to figure out which symbols your Bible is using. In the New American Bible (NAB), lowercase, italicized letters found in the text indicate a cross-reference, or where you can find another passage dealing with the same or related topic, story, character, etc. For example, if you were to read in the NAB version of the Gospel of John about Jesus' arrest, you will find at the end of Jn 18:1 a lowercase, italicized *n* indicating a cross-reference. In the list of cross-references, you will find that this same story or something related to it may be found in the following places:

2 Sm 15:23
Mt 26:30–36
Mk 14:26–32
Lk 22:39

By looking up the cross-references, you can compare how different books of the Bible tell the same story or echo a similar event. For example, if you read the following passage in Luke chapter 4 describing Jesus' appearance in the synagogue at Nazareth, notice

the indication of a cross-reference in the text that Jesus reads from
the scroll of Isaiah:

> 18 z*The spirit of the Lord is upon me,
> because he has anointed me
>   to bring glad tidings to the poor.
> He has sent me to proclaim liberty to captives
>   and recovery of sight to the blind,
>   to let the oppressed go free,
> 19and to proclaim a year acceptable to the Lord.

If you are a curious reader, you may ask yourself, "Where in
Isaiah can I find that passage?" Behold cross-reference z. In the
cross-reference section, look for the letter z. You'll find this cross-
reference: "Is 61:1–2; 58:6."

Because you know how to read Scripture citations properly
and can use your abbreviation list in the table of contents, you
know that you are looking for Isaiah chapter 61, verses 1 and 2.
Likewise, if you happen to be reading Is 61:1–2 and think to yourself, "This sounds familiar. Didn't Jesus say these words?" the
cross-reference on Is 61:1 will direct you to look at Lk 4:18. Isn't
that convenient?

Recall our earlier discussion about how different Bibles abbreviate books differently? The same caution needs to be made here
about cross-references and footnotes. Different translations or editions of the Bible may have a different approach to cross-
references. Some editions will list cross-references in the column
directly next to the text. Others will simply list cross-references at
the bottom of the page without using any symbols. Still others
may not even use cross-references at all. By the same token, different Bibles approach footnotes in a variety of ways. Some Bibles
footnote extensively, others very little. Some use symbols while

others use letters. The important thing is to read the introductory pages of your Bible to identify how that Bibles uses cross-references and footnotes.

Cross-references will send you traveling all over the Bible, enabling you to make more connections than the electrical wiring in your house. Much like footnotes, by using cross-references, you will be able to unleash the full power of God's word by opening doors from one passage to another and from one insight to another. To practice, look up the cross-references given in your Bible for the following gospel stories from Matthew:

- the birth of Jesus (Mt 1:20)

- the baptism of Jesus (Mt 3:13)

- the temptation of Jesus (Mt 4:1)

- the Golden Rule (Mt 7:12)

- Jesus feeds five thousand (Mt 14:13)

- the entry into Jerusalem (Mt 21:1)

- the Holy Eucharist (Mt 26:26)

- the agony in the garden (Mt 26:36)

- the women at the tomb (Mt 28:1)

But what happens when our footnotes and cross-references aren't enough?

Biblical Concordances and Dictionaries

Recall our earlier discussion of bibliaphobia. We addressed the idea that one of the reasons many of us are afraid of the Bible is its length. Most Bibles are between one and two thousand pages in length with miniscule print. Add to that the dizzying number of footnotes and cross-references, and each page can become quite involved. What's truly amazing is that despite all of the information given in the footnotes and cross-references, they only scratch the surface of the background information that could be given for each Scripture passage. If some kind of footnote or cross-reference were included for every name, date, and location in the Bible, it would increase the length of our Bibles from one or two thousand pages to ten or twenty thousand pages. For that reason, only the most essential information is given to us right in our Bibles. Additional information is available in what we call a biblical concordance (sometimes referred to as a dictionary-concordance). Today, a wide variety of biblical concordances are available not only in book form but also on CD-ROM. The following list is an example of the kinds of information you're likely to find in a concordance:

- literally tens of thousands of subject entries

- nearly a million words that occur in the Bible

- every name in the Bible

- descriptions of biblical places and of the daily life of the Hebrew people

- summaries of each book of the Bible

- historical background

At one time, biblical concordances were primarily a tool for Scripture scholars and theology majors. Today it is not necessary for the average Catholic to enroll in university theology classes to gain access to biblical information. Scholars have already done that work for us and have placed the fruits of their labor at our fingertips in these very valuable volumes, which are available at most bookstores. See the annotated bibliography for Catholic Scripture study on page 111 for suggested titles. With a concordance at our side, each time we read the Bible it is as though we have a Scripture scholar sitting beside us to answer our every question.

Biblical Commentaries

Finally, even with footnotes, cross-references, and concordance information, sometimes we still need assistance in understanding the meaning and significance of specific passages within the context of the whole chapter, book, testament, or Bible. At times like this, we need the assistance of biblical commentaries. Commentaries are essays that lead us chapter by chapter and verse by verse through each book of the Bible, providing us with a more detailed and holistic explanation of the Scripture passages we are reading. Commentaries are very helpful for those involved in Scripture study, preaching, pastoral ministry, or catechesis. However, personal prayer can be greatly enhanced as well by reading biblical commentaries. After reading a Scripture passage, it is often helpful to browse through a commentary before returning to the passage and prayerfully rereading it (more on how to prayerfully read the Bible in chapter 5). With the depth and background provided by the commentary, the word of God comes to life for us in a way that was not previously possible. Using a commentary to enhance our personal Scripture study and prayer is like plugging in an electrical device that previously did not work—the potential was there all along but the connection needed to be made! (See the annotated bibliography for Catholic Scripture study on page 111 for suggested titles.)

Using Your "Archeological" Tools

If we think of the Bible as a time capsule that contains valuable and meaningful treasures buried under centuries of dirt and mud, then we should think of footnotes, cross-references, concordances, and commentaries as the archeological tools we need to scrape away that which prevents us from encountering the full power of God's word. With these tools at our fingertips, we are now ready to forge ahead and make some startling discoveries about the Bible and how it can make a profound impact on our daily living.

QUESTIONS FOR REFLECTION AND DISCUSSION

- If you were to assemble a time capsule that captured the most significant and essential events, people, fads, news stories, and so on of the past year, what would you include?

- If you assembled such a time capsule, what might people 100 years from now have difficulty recognizing or understanding?

- Name something you have that is now obsolete but was considered state of the art only a short time ago.

- What part of the Bible have you had the most difficulty understanding?

- Browse through the Bible and search out a few footnotes. What is something you learned from reading a footnote that you did not know before?

- Do the same with a few cross-references. What is something you learned about a passage by comparing its cross-references?

- In what ways can a biblical concordance enhance your personal study of the Bible?

- How can biblical commentaries be of assistance to you in your understanding of the Bible?

Answer Key

1. c; 2. b; 3. b; 4. a; 5. d; 6. c; 7. a; 8. d; 9. a; 10. c.

FOUR

Truth or Fact?

So, then, is it true that . . .

• God created the world in seven days?

• Adam lived to be 930 years old?

• Noah built an ark and got two of *every* animal to board it?

• Jonah was swallowed by a large fish?

• The walls of Jericho fell at the blast of a trumpet?

• Samson lost all of his physical strength when he got his hair cut?

• David slew a giant named Goliath with a slingshot?

• Jesus survived forty days and forty nights in the desert without food?

- Tongues of fire appeared over the apostles on the feast of Pentecost?

- Only 144,000 will be saved at the end of the world?

How are we to understand the Bible? We may believe that the events listed above did happen (or will happen) just the way the Bible describes them. Such an approach affirms the awesome and almighty power of God, who can accomplish anything God wants. It may also lead us to wonder why such miraculous events no longer occur today in the same manner. Did God interact differently with the world in biblical times? On the other hand, we may conclude that these events did not occur exactly the way the Bible describes them and are "just stories." This conclusion explains why God seemed a little more "hands on" back then. Unfortunately, this approach may also lead us to conclude that the Bible is simply a collection of fables and fairy tales, to be lumped together with those of Aesop and the Brothers Grimm.

How we answer this question of "truth" is at the very core of our faith and our understanding of how God communicates with us in life as well as through sacred Scripture. Without any further ado, allow me to propose an answer that captures the essence of the Catholic approach to understanding the Bible: everything in the Bible is *true* . . . but not necessarily *fact*.

The way this answer is phrased is critical. Let there be no doubt that the Bible communicates the absolute truth of God. At the same time, understand that truth and fact are not the same thing! This answer is not meant to be tricky or gimmicky. It is intended to be a profound statement to all those who question whether or not the Bible is God's word or just a collection of stories. Make no mistake about it, the Bible is the word of God and everything in it is true.

Equally as important, this answer is offered as a more authentic, orthodox, and effective reply than the unfortunate and damaging "No, these things didn't really happen. They're just stories." Too many well-intentioned pastors, teachers, catechists, and pastoral ministers have used this reckless reply in their attempts to provide their students with a more mature and contemporary approach to the Bible. Instead of leading people to a deeper understanding of the Bible, the "they're just stories" approach minimizes the power of God's word, leading people to abandon the Bible.

Finally, the caveat included in the statement above ("but not necessarily *fact*") is directed at those who might espouse a fundamentalist (literal) approach to the Bible that would lead people to a narrow-minded approach to God's word. While a literal approach to the Bible expands the power of God in biblical stories, it creates a chasm between those stories and our own contemporary personal experience (i.e., God used to do things like part the waters of the Red Sea but doesn't anymore), thus minimizing the power of God in our everyday life. When we say that everything in the Bible is *true,* but not necessarily *fact,* we do not diminish the power of God in either the Bible or our experience. Likewise, we do not diminish the importance of the Bible but instead raise it up to a new height of importance, challenging readers and believers to approach it in a manner that no other literature is approached. God's Library is no ordinary library, and its contents cannot be understood in the same way that other books are understood.

Understanding Myth in a Literal Society

In order to truly understand the Bible, we need to go back and understand the culture in which it was written—a culture that understood stories and the concept of myth in a much different way than we tend to understand them today. We live in a very literal culture. Through science, we have the power to prove almost anything. If something cannot be proven, it is considered false. Today, when we refer to something as a story, we are suggesting that what is being communicated is not true. Likewise, our use of the word *myth* carries very negative connotations. When someone concocts a tall tale, we call it a myth. As a result, the word *myth* is almost synonymous with the word *lie* or *falsehood*.

Not so in biblical culture.

The difference between contemporary cultures and cultures of biblical times can be traced to an understanding of the differences between truth and fact. In the cultures of biblical times, stories and myth were seen as the vehicles by which the most essential and sacred truths of a people were communicated and passed on. Scientific proof was not available, nor was it needed in order to pass on what the heart held as absolute and essential. Today, unless something is substantiated by facts, we consider it false. In biblical times, truth could be conveyed whether or not the facts were all straight. For this reason, it is critical for Bible readers to rely on the insights of Scripture scholars who can shed light on the original author's intent and help us sort out what was intended to be presented as fact and what wasn't. We'll talk more about this in the next chapter.

Since society in biblical times did not base its sense of truth on literal interpretation, facts were often of secondary importance. In other words, biblical cultures understood that something can be true but need not be a fact! At first, this may sound outrageous, but a closer look at our own culture and use of language reveals that we know exactly how to find truth in something that isn't factual. Read the following paragraph and pay attention to the phrases in italics.

My kids are *driving me up the wall.* There I was trying to get to church on time and these little *rugrats* were *tearing up the place.* I was *pulling my hair out* to keep some kind of order in the house and they didn't *give a hoot.* To *top it all off,* when we left the house, it was *raining cats and dogs.* Since I had left my umbrella at work, *I was up the creek without a paddle.* So I had to *hotfoot* it to the car while *juggling* these two kids. Naturally, we *drowned.* Then, when we got to within a block of church, this train with a *billion* cars *crawled* across the street at about *two feet an hour. I blew my top.* After waiting there about *three days,* we finally got to church and sat down just as Father was giving a talk about getting to church on time. *I just about died!*

What you've just read is a true story, in that the events described truly occurred. However, many of the phrases used to describe these events are not at all factual. As long as you understand the use of figurative language, you have no problem accepting the story as true. You would never pause to ask, "Is it true that cats and dogs were falling from the sky?" The use of the phrase *cats and dogs* conveys truth without using fact. As long as you understand figurative language, the hyperbole of the language doesn't faze you. It is this understanding of figurative language that allows us to conclude that everything in the Bible is true, but not everything in the Bible is a fact! With this in mind, let's take a closer look at some examples from Scripture.

Is it true that Adam lived to be 930 years old? If you understand that the biblical authors use age in the Hebrew Scriptures to make a point, you'll get it. In Jewish culture (as in many others), to live a long life is considered to be a blessing from God. Adam, who was the father of all, was truly blessed and his age represents that. As the stories in Genesis continue on, the ages decrease as the sinfulness of humankind escalates. The use of age here is not intended to represent fact but to convey truth: God's blessing is gradually being rejected by men and women who are in need of salvation.

Is it true that Noah built an ark and got one or two of every species of animal on board to survive a flood that washed out all of humankind? There may very well have been a flood and an ark. Consider this: because of mass communication and technology, our world has been transformed into a global village. When something happens on one side of the world, the rest of the world can watch it on the news. In primitive cultures, this was not true. The world's boundaries were limited by the limited knowledge of geography. A devastating flood could easily have wiped out the "world" as it was known at the time by a particular culture. Such tragedies were always seen as punishment from God. Perhaps a just man named Noah did survive with his family and his farm animals. What we do know for sure is that this is a true story. The story teaches us the sacred and essential truth that humankind will drown in sinfulness. The only thing that will keep one afloat is to live an upright life. Sinfulness is punished and goodness is saved. God replenishes that which God has created. Perhaps some day, someone will find Noah's ark and prove that the story is indeed factual. In the meantime, we already know that it's true.

Is it true that the Garden of Eden exists? In the book of Genesis, we are told that the Garden of Eden exists where four rivers meet: the Pishon, the Gihon, the Tigris, and the Euphrates. All you need to do is discover where these four rivers meet and you will have discovered the Garden of Eden. The only problem is that these four rivers do not meet. Is the Bible lying to us? Is the Bible false? No. These four rivers *do* meet . . . in the land of myth. The biblical author is alerting us to the fact that the following story is *sacred*. The reader is being forewarned: prepare to enter into sacred space and confront an essential truth of life.

Is it true that God created the world in seven days? If we believe the creation story literally, what do we do about the "big bang" and evolution? If we believe the big bang theory and the theory of evolution, does that make the Bible's version false? No. We don't have to take sides. The Bible story of creation in seven days is a true story. Likewise, the second story of creation found in Genesis chapter 2 is *also* true. The Bible itself gives us two stories—which is true? They both are. Even though the *facts* of the two stories conflict, they both teach us sacred and essential truths: creation comes from God; all of creation is good and blessed; man and woman are made in the image of God; humankind is responsible for caring for creation; and the idea of resting once per week is divine. As for the facts concerning the actual process of creation, we don't know. We weren't there when it happened. However, the biblical stories of creation and the scientific theories of the big bang and evolution are not mutually exclusive. As one bumper sticker puts it: "The Big Bang Theory: God said BANG! and it happened!"

Is it true that Jonah was swallowed by a large fish? Like every story in the Bible, we need to remind ourselves that the story of Jonah is not just about a character that lived long ago and far away; it is our story. Every Bible story is somehow the story of your life and my life. The story of Jonah is not a story about whether a man can factually survive in the belly of a large fish for three days, but a story about what happens when you and I try to run away from God's call and God's will. Jonah was called by God to preach to the people of Nineveh and call them to repentance. He didn't want to do that. So, in the great tradition of Adam and Eve, he tried to run and hide. This story teaches us a sacred and essential truth of life: you can run but you can't hide from God. Jonah boards a ship, is blamed for causing a storm to erupt because he disobeyed his God, and is tossed overboard only to be swallowed by a large fish. It is while he's in the belly of the large fish that conversion happens to Jonah. Large fish bellies have a way of doing that to people. After three days and three nights (pay attention to the use of numbers . . . more on that coming up soon), Jonah has a change of heart and proceeds to call the people of Nineveh to repentance. This true story teaches us that when we run from God, we encounter storms, darkness, and isolation, and that in our isolation, God can and will find us. God does not give up easily. Once, after I explained to a group of adults how the Jonah story is true though not necessarily fact, a woman came up to me with tears in her eyes. She said that she understood what it meant to be in the belly of the large fish. She was in a twelve-step program recovering from an addiction and said that hitting rock bottom and being in complete darkness was like being in the belly of the large fish. Now, she realized that if she followed God's will instead of trying to run and hide from it, conversion would be possible. She knew without a doubt that the Jonah story is true. She recognized that the miracle in the story is not that God once provided a huge fish to swallow Jonah, but that God can change your heart, if you stop running.

Is it true that Jesus went forty days and forty nights in the desert without eating any food? Jesus is the Son of God and can perform miracles beyond explanation. At the same time, he is fully human. No human can survive a month and ten days in the desert without some kind of food. Yet, this is a true story. We mentioned a few moments ago that it's important to pay attention to the use of numbers in the Bible. Here we have forty days and forty nights (where have you seen this number used before?). The number forty is highly symbolic. It communicates the idea of a significant period of time. Recall that the people of Israel passed through the waters of the Red Sea and spent forty years wandering through the desert, often tempted because of lack of food. Jesus now has passed through the waters of his baptism and is led into the desert, where he too is tempted. Israel failed their test. Jesus is triumphant. The truth of this story is that for a significant period of time, reminiscent of the time that Israel spent in the desert, Jesus faced temptation regarding mankind's true source of nourishment and well-being. He resists temptation and places his trust in the Father, who alone is the source of all that sustains us, body and soul. We too have crossed through the waters of baptism and endure significant periods of dryness during which we grapple with the question of our true source of nourishment and well-being. Jesus' experience provides us with the answer.

Was it light or was it dark? The Gospel of Mark tells us that the women came to the tomb on that first Easter morning "very early when the sun had risen" (Mk 16:2). The Gospel of John tells us that they came upon the tomb "while it was still dark" (Jn 20:1). This conflict may cause us trouble if we are looking for the literal time of the Resurrection. When did they come to the tomb? If the sun had risen, it would be bright and not still dark. Which story is true? They both are. The Gospel of John uses the images of light and dark throughout: "the light shines in the darkness" (1:5), "whoever lives the truth comes to the light" (3:21), "I am the light of the world" (9:5), "I came into the world as light" (12:46). It makes sense to have the women arrive at the tomb "while it was still dark," to reinforce the image that the people who "walked in darkness" will soon see "a great light!" (also reminiscent of Isaiah 9:1). The fact that these two stories describe the same event, yet use different "facts" reinforces the notion that the authors are not as concerned with literal facts as we are today, but are instead concerned with communicating the truth: namely, that Jesus, the light of the world, is risen.

Was it on the mount or on the plain? We are all familiar with Jesus' famous discourse referred to as the Beatitudes (i.e., "Blessed are the poor in spirit . . ."). Interestingly enough, Matthew's Gospel tells us that Jesus delivered this sermon on "the mountain" (mount) while Luke's Gospel tells us that it was delivered on "level ground" (plain). Simply put, a mount is not a plain. Which story is true? Once again, both. The authors are not concerned with the fact of where Jesus stood, but instead with the truth of his teaching. Matthew's Gospel is written for an audience that was primarily Jewish. A Jewish audience would need a great deal of convincing to believe that Jesus was a greater prophet than Moses. What better way to do this than to have Jesus deliver his new "commandments" from atop a mountain, just as Moses received the Ten Commandments on Mount Sinai? The facts of where Jesus actually stood are overpowered by the truth being communicated here: Jesus is a prophet far greater than even Moses.

References to Numbers and Locations

As you read the Bible, pay close attention to the use of numbers and locations. References to such "facts" are often a clue to some deeper symbolic meaning. While archeology has substantiated many historical, geographical, and numerical references in the Bible, quite often the authors were not as interested in the facts as we tend to be, but were instead using numbers and locations as a tool for communicating something symbolic. Let's take a closer look at each of these.

NUMBERS

The biblical authors loved numbers. Some numbers are good. Some are bad. Some numbers are repeated so often that we can rightly become a bit suspicious. We've already talked a little about the number forty. How often do we see this number? Well, guess what the answer is to all of the following questions:

- How many days and nights did it rain for Noah?

- How many days did it take to embalm Jacob?

- How many years old were Jacob and Esau when they each got married?

- How many years did the Israelites wander through the desert?

- How many years did both David and Solomon rule as king?

- How many years old was Moses when he slew an Egyptian?

- How many years later did Moses encounter the burning bush?

- How many days was Moses on the mountaintop before he came down with the commandments?

- How many days did it take Moses' scouts to reconnoiter the land of Canaan?

- How many days and nights did Goliath take his stand before meeting up with David?

- How many days and nights did Elijah walk strengthened by the food and drink he received?

- How many days' warning did Jonah give the people of Nineveh?

- How many days and nights did Jesus spend in the desert without food?

- How many days did Jesus remain with his disciples after his resurrection?

The answer to all of the above: forty. In fact, the number forty occurs more than eighty times in the Bible. This is a clue that it is being used as a symbol and not strictly to communicate fact. Deuteronomy 8:2 tells us about the significance of the number forty. "Remember how for forty years now the LORD, your God, has directed all your journeying in the desert, so as to test you by affliction and find out whether or not it was your intention to keep his commandments."

In other words, the number forty represents a significant period of time during which a person's faithfulness is tested and can be judged or determined. Other numbers are used frequently in the Bible to convey symbolic meaning. Here are a few more examples.

3

The number three appears hundreds of times in the Bible. In biblical tradition, it is always on the third day that God saves. The angel intervened to stop Abraham from sacrificing Isaac on the third day. After three days in the desert without water, God provided fresh water through Moses. The prophet Hosea says, "He will revive us after two days; / on the third day he will raise us up, / to live in his presence" (Hos 6:2). Jonah emerged from the large fish on the third day. Paul regained his sight on the third day. Mary and Joseph found the twelve-year-old Jesus in the temple on the third day. Jesus fed 4,000 people after they had been with him for three days with nothing to eat. Jesus rose from the dead on the third day. The book of Exodus gives us a clue about the significance of the third day when it says, "Go to the people . . . make them wash their garments and be ready for the third day; for on the third day the LORD will come down on Mount Sinai before the eyes of all the people . . . On the morning of the third day there were peals of thunder and lightning, and a heavy cloud over the mountain, and a very loud trumpet blast, so that all the people in the camp trembled . . . for the LORD came down upon it in fire" (Ex 19:10–11, 16, 18). Needless to say, the number three is one of those "good" numbers in the Bible because God always comes through on the third day.

6

The number six, on the other hand, is not such a good number. Not that it's bad, but it tends to represent incompleteness. Noah was 600 years old when the flood came. Pharaoh sent 600 first-class chariots to chase after the Israelites. God worked for six days to create the heavens and the earth but blessed and made holy the seventh day for rest. Of course, in the book of Revelation, the "beast" is represented by the number 666. Think about that: three is a good number, representing completeness. Six represents *in*completeness. Three sixes, or 666, represents complete incompleteness! In other words, the use of 666 in the book of Revelation is not some secret code to tell us who the Antichrist will be. It is simply a symbolic way of representing evil in whatever form it may take in any age.

7

The number seven . . . ah, back to the good numbers. Seven tends to represent fullness or perfection. God rested on the seventh day. Noah took seven pairs of all clean animals aboard the ark. The walls of Jericho came tumbling down after seven days of trumpet playing. Jesus tells Peter to forgive his brother seventy times seven times. The book of Revelation speaks to the seven churches. The same book also tells us that the seventh trumpet will signal the end of the world. Whenever we encounter the number seven, it tends to be satisfying.

12

Last but not least is the number twelve. Twelve, of course, symbolizes first and foremost the fullness of the people of Israel, with its twelve tribes. The people of Israel discovered an oasis called Elim with twelve streams of water. Jesus, of course, had twelve apostles. And, once again, the book of Revelation tops it all off by telling us that 144,000 people will be saved at the end of the world, a number that is divisible by twelve, representing twelve thousand from each of the twelve tribes of Israel. With this much use of the number twelve, we can be sure that we are dealing with metaphorical language and not facts. In other words, we don't know how many people will be saved at the end of the world, but the truth is that God's work will have reached its completion.

The bottom line to all this is that numbers are a clue to the reader: pay attention and look for the deeper meaning. Look for the truth being communicated.

LOCATIONS

Many biblical references to locations have proven to be histori-
cally accurate. Archeologists have unearthed cities referred to in
the Old Testament that were thought to be fictional or at least
long gone. Many locations referred to still exist, some in a rela-
tively unchanged state. On the other hand, we encounter many
other references to locations that prove troublesome. We've
already discussed the problem of the location of the Garden of
Eden and the question of whether Jesus delivered the Beatitudes
on a mount or on a plain. More questions may arise as we read.
Was Jesus really born in Bethlehem? Did the Holy Family really
hide in Egypt? Did Jesus travel to Jerusalem once as Matthew,
Mark, and Luke tell us or three times as John indicates? (Notice
the use of the number three here?) Why were the two disciples on
the road to a place called Emmaus after Jesus' death?

The key here is to recall our discussion of the difference
between truth and fact. The biblical authors were concerned with
teaching truth. They were not historians or geographers, and their
use of locations is often as symbolic as their use of numbers.
Locations conjure up images. Even today when someone names a
location, people have a reaction, either positive or negative depending on what that location suggests. How are we to know how
people in biblical times reacted to certain locations? Often, footnotes and commentaries will contain useful information. For now,
here are a few clues about some places that we just mentioned.

Bethlehem The prophet Micah refers to Bethlehem saying,
"But you, Bethlehem-Ephrathah, / too small to be among the
clans of Judah, / From you shall come forth for me / one who is
to be ruler in Israel" (Mi 5:1). When the Gospels of Matthew and

Luke tell us that Jesus was born in Bethlehem, they are teaching us the truth that Jesus is the ruler who has come from humble beginnings to become the shepherd of all Israel, thus fulfilling the hopes and expectations of God's people.

Egypt The Gospel of Matthew is the only Gospel that recounts the flight into Egypt. Recall that Matthew was writing for a predominantly Jewish audience familiar with the story of the Exodus. To such an audience, this reference would immediately summon images of the time that God called forth his people out of the land of Egypt. In the same way, Jesus would now be seen as called by God out of the land of Egypt to form a new people. While there is much we don't know about Jesus' early life, we do know this: Jesus is the one called by God to emancipate the new Israel (that means you and me) from the sin that enslaves us, and lead us to the Promised Land of our salvation.

Jesus' Travels to Jerusalem Matthew, Mark, and Luke tell us that Jesus "cleansed" the temple during his last days as part of his only journey to Jerusalem. John places this event near the beginning of his ministry and has Jesus returning to Jerusalem a total of three times. These facts seem to conflict. The truth is, however, that Jerusalem and the temple were seen as the center of Jewish life. John's Gospel was written at a time when Jewish Christians were experiencing the turmoil of being thrown out of their synagogues as the split between Jews and Jewish Christians deepened and grew acrimonious. John's chronology of Jesus' three visits to Jerusalem and his references to the cleansing of the temple at the beginning of Jesus' ministry emphasize the truth that Jesus is the new center of God's presence in the world, replacing the temple in Jerusalem that the Christians of John's time no longer had access to. And since God saves on the third day, it makes sense that Jesus' saving action—his death and resurrection—would occur on his third visit to Jerusalem.

Emmaus Where the heck is Emmaus, and why are two disciples headed there after Jesus' tragic death? The fact is, very little is known about Emmaus. It seems to have absolutely no significance, and that's the point. After Jesus' death, the disciples were lost and directionless. The only important thing about the location of Emmaus is that the two disciples are headed *away* from Jerusalem. The disciples are attempting to leave behind the experience of Jesus' death. They don't know where they are headed as long as it is away from the past. After their encounter with the risen Jesus on the road to Emmaus, their destination changes: they make a 180-degree turn and head back to Jerusalem, back to where Jesus' death occurred. While we know little about a place called Emmaus, we do know the truth: when we are lost and without direction, we do not recognize the presence of the risen Lord in our midst. When we do encounter him in the sharing of God's word and the breaking of the bread, our eyes are opened, and we can revisit the place of our pain with a new faith.

Personally, my favorite "location" reference is a little-known one found in the sixth chapter of Mark's Gospel. The chapter begins with Jesus and his disciples in Nazareth. Jesus encounters some difficulty in his own town. He proceeds to send out the twelve. After they come back reporting their success, Jesus invites them to an out-of-the-way place, a deserted region not far from the shore of the Sea of Galilee. In this deserted place, Jesus feeds 5,000 people despite the apostles' reluctance. All of this is taking place on the western shore of the Sea of Galilee: Jewish territory. After this incident, Jesus tells the apostles to get in the boat and precede him to the other side of the lake toward Bethsaida . . . gentile territory. That evening, the apostles do so, but encounter their own turbulence as they try to row with the wind against them. Between three and six in the morning (note: they've been rowing since evening . . . a total of between nine and twelve hours), Jesus comes walking on the water toward them. After he gets in the boat and the winds calm down, the story tells us the following: "After making the crossing, they came to land at Gennesaret" (Mk 6:53). Interestingly enough, Gennesaret is on the western shore of the Sea of Galilee, which is where they were before they left! After struggling all night rowing against the wind for nine to twelve hours, they ended up just about back where they started.

We tend to miss all of this symbolism because we are not familiar with the area around the Sea of Galilee. However, audiences familiar with the region would certainly catch the irony in the apostles' destination. Is the author trying to give us historical information about location? Perhaps. But more important, the author is using references to location in order to communicate some very important truths: the twelve apostles (the "church") had a difficult time carrying the gospel across the lake to unfamiliar territory. They could make no headway in the face of turbulence. Only Jesus can rise above this (walking on the water). Jesus alone leads them on to Tyre and Sidon and the district of the Ten Cities, all gentile areas where, interestingly enough, in chapter 8 of Mark's Gospel, he again feeds a huge crowd, this time 4,000 people, after they had been with him three days. All of these references to location reinforce the powerful messages in these stories . . . all of which are true.

"But I Need to Have Proof!"

Once, when I was delivering a God's Library workshop to a group of young adults in a Chicago suburb, I covered the above examples of figurative language in the Bible and the difference between truth and fact. While the participants listened intently and accepted the approach I was taking, two main concerns surfaced. One was, "if the Bible is not all fact and uses figurative language and stories, that opens the door for anyone to interpret them any way they so desire!" The fact is, we are called upon to interpret the Bible in light of our experiences. However, we do so within a broader tradition of interpretation going back over 2,000 years. This tradition of interpretation invites us to consider the original context in which a passage was written as well as the original author's intent. We simply cannot understand the full meaning of a Bible passage for ourselves today until we have some insight into its meaning as originally intended. It is also important to remember that while the Bible speaks to us personally it does not speak to us exclusively. We are not free to interpret the Bible any old way we please, but within the context of our Catholic Christian tradition. Our interpretation of the Bible must be done in communion with our present-day brothers and sisters in the church as well as with those who have gone before us marked with the sign of faith.

The second concern was even more pointed. One participant applied all of this discussion of figurative language to the story of the Resurrection and said, "I understand how this might apply to Noah's ark or some other ancient story, but I have to know that Jesus literally rose from the dead. I need proof of that!" I responded first by stating emphatically that we do know for a fact that Jesus was a historical person. Then, I stated that without a doubt, I believe that Jesus is risen. Yet, that absolute confidence is based on testimony, not proof. No one can offer proof of the Resurrection. Not even the Bible offers proof. What we do have are the astonishing accounts of those who proclaim that their lives were completely transformed by an encounter with the one they recognized as the risen Jesus. Their stories are overwhelmingly compelling—compelling enough to change the lives of millions of people over the last 2,000 years.

The Resurrection is something we believe in by faith, based on powerful evidence and testimony of witnesses. Such evidence, although powerful and compelling, falls short of proof. Each time we celebrate the Eucharist, we say, "Let us proclaim the *mystery* of our faith: Christ has died, Christ is risen, Christ will come again!" Ultimately, the Bible does not provide us with proof of anything. And yet, we can read it with absolute confidence, knowing that we can trust God, who is good to his word. The Bible provides us with the compelling testimony of those who have encountered the risen Christ, been transformed, and now invite us to enter into his paschal mystery. In his book *Against an Infinite Horizon,* Ronald Rolheiser explains that "certitude is not the real substance of faith. Faith is a way of seeing things" (9). Ultimately, Scripture helps us to see our lives, not in isolation, but against the backdrop of Jesus' paschal mystery. Robert Ludwig describes in his book *Reconstructing Catholicism: For a New Generation* how the Bible (the Gospels, in particular) does this. "It is our story, it is the story of all the earth, a universal story about gracious mystery as our source and destiny and the need to live by courage and trust. Yet, this story is not an 'answer' to our questions, as the fundamentalists would have it. Rather, the Gospel is the thematization of our experience of mystery, helping us make peace with our deepest questions by our acceptance of incompleteness, vulnerability, emptiness" (97).

Finally, it is important here to lend credibility to this whole discussion about the difference between truth and fact. In other words, the approach to Scripture described in this chapter is not something that I made up. Rather, it is a summary of the official position of the Catholic Church as expressed by the Pontifical

Biblical Commission's document entitled "The Interpretation of the Bible in the Church." Here are a few quotations from that document that serve as the foundation for this chapter.

> Fundamentalism places undue stress upon the inerrancy of certain details in the biblical texts, especially in what concerns historical events or supposedly scientific truth. It often historicizes material which from the start never claimed to be historical. It considers historical everything that is reported or recounted with verbs in the past tense, failing to take the necessary account of the possibility of symbolic or figurative meaning.

It is not sufficient to translate a text word for word in order to obtain its literal sense. One must understand the text according to the literary conventions of the time. When a text is metaphorical, its literal sense is not that which flows immediately from a word-to-word translation (e.g., "Let your loins be girt": Lk 12:35), but that which corresponds to the metaphorical use of these terms ("Be ready for action"). When it is a question of a story, the literal sense does not necessarily imply belief that the facts recounted actually took place, for a story need not belong to the genre of history but be instead a work of imaginative fiction.

Fundamentalism refuses to admit that the inspired word of God has been expressed in human language and that this word has been expressed, under divine inspiration, by human authors possessed of limited capacities and resources. For this reason, it tends to treat the biblical text as if it had been dictated word for word by the Spirit. It fails to recognize that the word of God has been formulated in language and expression conditioned by various periods.

The fundamentalist approach is dangerous, for it is attractive to people who look to the Bible for ready answers to the problems of life. It can deceive these people, offering them interpretations that are pious but illusory, instead of telling them that the Bible does not necessarily contain an immediate answer to each and every problem. Without saying as much in so many words, fundamentalism actually invites people to a kind of intellectual suicide. It injects into life a false certitude, for it unwittingly confuses the divine substance of the biblical message with what are in fact its human limitations.

Fundamentalism is right to insist on the divine inspiration of the Bible, the inerrancy of the word of God, and other biblical truths included in its five fundamental points. But its way of presenting these truths is rooted in an ideology that is not biblical, whatever the proponents of this approach might say. For it demands an unshakable adherence to rigid doctrinal points of view and imposes, as the only source of teaching for Christian life and salvation, a reading of the Bible that rejects all questioning and any kind of critical research.

It does not follow from this pontifical document that we can attribute to a biblical text whatever meaning we like, interpreting it in a wholly subjective way. On the contrary, one must reject as inauthentic every interpretation alien to the meaning expressed by the human authors in their written text.

In its attachment to the principle "Scripture alone," fundamentalism separates the interpretation of the Bible from the tradition, which, guided by the Spirit, has authentically developed in union with Scripture in the heart of the community of faith. It presents itself as a form of private interpretation that does not acknowledge that the church is founded on the Bible and draws its life and inspiration from Scripture.

The approach to Scripture that I've presented in this book is an authentic Catholic approach to understanding the Bible as articulated by the Vatican's Pontifical Biblical Commission.

QUESTIONS FOR REFLECTION AND DISCUSSION

- In your own words describe the difference between truth and fact. What are some examples from everyday language?

- A clever Scripture professor once said, "Everything in the Bible is true . . . and some of them actually happened." What does this mean? How does it compare with the statement we've used ("Everything in the Bible is true, but not necessarily fact")?

• After reading this chapter, how would you respond to someone who asks you a question like "Did Adam and Eve really exist?" or "Was there really a Noah's ark?"

• After reading this chapter, how would you respond to someone who accuses you of making the Bible sound like a fairy tale by all this talk about the difference between truth and fact?

• For a good laugh, rent the movie *Airplane* and make a list of all the figurative language that is portrayed literally. Use this as an exercise in illustrating how complex language can be. For children, locate a copy of *Amelia Bedelia,* which also illustrates how comical it can be to take something literally that is meant to be understood figuratively.

• How are numbers and locations used for effect in Bible stories? What are some examples?

• What does the Pontifical Biblical Commission teach us about understanding the Bible in "The Interpretation of the Bible in the Church"? How do you feel about the approach to understanding the Bible proposed by this chapter and this document? How does this approach change your understanding of the Bible? How does it help? How does it challenge?

FIVE

Interpreting and Applying
the Bible

In the Polish language, a good meal is often associated with the word *Smacznego!* (smoch-NEH-go). What does it mean in English? Well, before a meal, it means something similar to *bon apetite*. During or after a meal, it means "delicious." Or, perhaps it means, "Mmmmmm." Then again, maybe it really means, "That was great." Unfortunately, the English language doesn't really have a word that exactly captures the essence of *smacznego*. In other words, if you ask several different people what *smacznego* means in English, you may get several different answers depending upon one's interpretation. When we go from one language to another, we need to interpret what we believe the original language is attempting to say.

What does this have to do with the Bible? Well, first and foremost, the Bible was *not* written in English (neither did Jesus speak English). When people get nervous about "interpreting" the Bible, they have to realize that every Bible that is not written in the original language of the author *is* an interpretation. Most biblical texts were originally written in Hebrew or Greek. By the third century, the Old Testament books originally written in

Hebrew were translated into Greek, and by the fifth century, the entire Bible was translated into Latin. As centuries progressed, the Bible was translated into dozens of languages. In other words, when someone gets upset about "contemporary" translations of the Bible, insisting that we use the "original" text (usually meaning the King James Version), they had better be prepared to read either Hebrew or Greek because there is no such thing as the *original English* text.

Every Bible is an interpretation of the original text. Therefore, we need not be afraid of the word *interpretation* when it comes to the Bible. We are called to interpret the Bible within the context of our faith tradition and within the context of the author's original intent, as well as we are able to ascertain that through scholarly research. Let's take a closer look at how we interpret the Bible as a faith community and as an individual within that faith community.

How Do I Choose a Bible?

If different Bibles employ different interpretations, how can one select a Bible that is consistent with a Catholic approach to the word of God? First, we need to understand the difference between Catholic and Protestant Bibles. While both are the inspired word of God, it is important to note that our two traditions have different "floor plans" for organizing God's Library. Both the Catholic and Protestant traditions have developed their own final list of which books are considered inspired and thus to be included in the Bible. This final official list is referred to as the canon. The Catholic canon contains the seventy-three books we outlined earlier in this book: forty-six Old Testament and twenty-seven New Testament. The Protestant canon includes sixty-six books, excluding seven Old Testament books: Tobit, Judith, Wisdom, Sirach

(Ecclesiasticus), Baruch, and First and Second Maccabees. Why the difference?

In the first century after Christ, rabbis in Palestine gathered to form the canon of the Hebrew Scriptures. They selected only those thirty-nine books that were written in Hebrew and had existed for what they considered to be a significant period of time. Around the same time, however, Greek-speaking Jews were using an Old Testament canon made up of forty-six books, including some books that were written in Greek or were of a more recent authorship than those in the Hebrew canon. Early Christians used both the Hebrew canon and the Greek canon. Although the early church included these seven books as part of the canon, opinion was divided regarding their canonical status. St. Jerome, who translated the Bible into Latin in the fifth century (his translation is called the Vulgate), referred to these seven books as the apocrypha, meaning "hidden." Although he included these books in his translation, he considered them to be outside of the canon. Thus, for many centuries, the exact standing of these seven Old Testament books continued to be called into question by some. During the Reformation in the sixteenth century, Protestants established a canon of thirty-nine Old Testament books, using only those books recognized as canonical by the first-century Jews and dismissing the apocryphal books. From this came the King James Version, which remained the standard biblical text in English until the twentieth century. Meanwhile, the Catholic Church at the Council of Trent (1546) definitively affirmed the seven "apocryphal" books as part of the canon, referring to them as "deuterocanonical," which means a "second" canon. Thus, the deuterocanonical books are those whose scriptural character, once contested, have been affirmed as part of the canon of the Bible.

So, the first thing to know about the differences between Catholic and Protestant Bibles is in terms of which books are included. However, using this rule on its own can be tricky because many Protestant publishers, eager to get a share in the growing market for Catholic Bible readership, are now including the deuterocanonical books in their Bible editions. This leads us to a second way the two types of Bible versions differ—in the content of the support materials, study helps, and learning tools, such as footnotes and commentaries. When these support materials venture into the area of doctrine, the differences between a Catholic Bible and a Protestant Bible can be profound. For example, support materials in a Protestant Bible may make reference to the recognition of two, and only two, sacraments: baptism and the Lord's Supper. Catholics, of course, recognize seven sacraments. Some Protestant Bibles include support materials that take a fundamentalist approach not in keeping with the Catholic approach we covered in the last chapter. Finally, a few Protestant Bibles (e.g., the Scofield Bible, the Tyndale Bible) can include support materials that are blatantly anti-Catholic. So, if you are seeking an interpretation of biblical texts that is in line with Catholic tradition, it is best to use a Catholic Bible.

Well into the twentieth century, the only Catholic versions of the Bible were translated from St. Jerome's Latin version of the fifth century. In 1943, Pope Pius XII called for a Catholic translation based on the earliest available manuscripts and the *original* languages. Since that time, several translations have been made under Catholic sponsorship. However, just because a Bible has the word *Catholic* on it (such as the New Living Translation: Catholic Reference Edition by Tyndale House) does not mean that it has been approved for Catholic audiences. The best way to determine if a Bible is approved for Catholic readership is to look for what is called an imprimatur (im-pri-MAH-tur) near the inside cover of a Bible. The imprimatur, followed by the name of the Roman Catholic authority issuing it, indicates that the translation is acceptable for use by Roman Catholics.

Which translation do we use at Mass on Sundays? The New American Bible (NAB) is the translation that we hear proclaimed at Mass in the United States. It makes sense to use this translation in your own studies and prayer since it will be reinforced at Sunday liturgy. A very popular version of the New American Bible is the Catholic Study Bible, which provides extensive footnotes and commentary. Another very popular Catholic Bible is the New Jerusalem Bible (NJB). The NJB was translated primarily by Catholic scholars in Great Britain. Another version that is more ecumenical in the makeup of its Scripture scholars but still carries an imprimatur is the New Revised Standard Version (NRSV). Rather than attempting to provide an exhaustive guide to selecting Bibles, know that if a Bible carries an imprimatur, it is considered acceptable for Catholic readership.

Recognizing Different Types of Literature

When you pick up the mail each day, what do you do? Most likely, you sort it out—some are pieces of junk mail, some are bills, some are personal letters, etc. You can usually identify what type of mail is contained within just by looking at the outside of the envelopes. The way you read each piece of mail depends on how you've sorted and identified it. Junk mail gets tossed with nary a glance while personal mail may be read over and over (and kept under your pillow at night!). The more mail you get (and the older and wiser you become), the better able you become at identifying what type of mail it is you are about to read. You even learn not to be fooled by the envelopes that tell you that you may have just won $10,000,000.

One of the first steps involved in interpreting the Bible is to learn to identify just what type of literature it is that you are reading. Like sorting out the morning mail, you can separate different types of biblical literature into different categories. Just as we do not read all of our mail in the same way, we do not read every type of biblical literature in the same manner. The more we read the Bible, the better we will become at differentiating a parable from a proverb, a genealogy from a discourse, a psalm from a letter, and a prophecy from a legal code.

The key to determining what type of literature you are reading in the Bible is to look at what you're reading within its broader context. The introduction to the book you are reading will often tell you what type of literature you are about to encounter. Likewise, the footnotes we discussed earlier will often reveal secrets about the type of literature under scrutiny. Finally, any Scripture passage must be interpreted in light of its broader context, namely in relation to the preceding and following chapters and verses.

Let's take a look at an example. Suppose we were reading the following passage:

> As in all the churches of the holy ones, women should keep silent in the churches, for they are not allowed to speak, but should be subordinate, as even the law says. But if they want to learn anything, they should ask their husbands at home. For it is improper for a woman to speak in the church.
> (1 Cor 14:33–35)

What are we to make of a passage like this? If we take this passage literally and isolated from its context, we can conclude that women should not be allowed any speaking roles in our celebrations of the Eucharist. But we know this is not true because women and men participate in all of the spoken responses of the Mass. Likewise, women may serve as lectors, proclaiming God's word to the assembly. Let's take a look at some key questions we must ask any time we attempt to properly interpret Scripture.

What type of literature is this? If we go back to the title of the book that this passage is taken from, we find that we are reading from the first *letter* of Paul to the Corinthians. This means that we are reading a letter written to a specific group of people who lived in Corinth during the first century AD. We need to understand the general purpose of Paul's letters and the role they played in the early church. When we recognize this literature as a letter, we recognize that we need to get the flavor of the whole letter before we isolate specific verses.

What do we know of the author? In many books of the Bible, we do not know precisely who the author was. In this passage, we are fortunate enough to know that St. Paul is the writer. The more we know about St. Paul's style of writing and his theology, the better we are able to interpret passages from his work. Paul was not afraid to speak his mind and felt very strongly about the need for order in the community.

Who was the "target audience" for this work? Who were the people of Corinth? In order to understand this passage, we need to learn a little bit about the people it was addressed to. Depending on the Bible version you are using, there may be some good background information on audience in the introduction to 1 Corinthians. In this example, we discover that the church of Corinth had many problems. Paul felt it was his responsibility to address these problems in a straightforward manner to achieve order in the community.

What is the overall thrust of the chapter? of the book? Taken in isolation, we can conclude that this passage compels us to forbid women to speak in church. However, when we look at the overall context of Paul's first letter to the Corinthians, we find that Paul seems to be contradicting some earlier statements he made about the role of women at worship. In chapter 11 verse 5, Paul writes that "any woman who prays or prophesies with her head unveiled brings shame upon her head." Here, Paul clearly is addressing the possibility of women speaking in liturgical leadership roles. When we return to 14:34–35, we find upon close examination that Paul is referring to the notion of women *asking questions* during the liturgy, ("if they want to learn anything, they should ask their husbands at home"). He is not suggesting here that women have no role in worship. He is talking about keeping order in the assembly. In fact, the overall context of this chapter and the whole book reveals that Paul is trying to establish liturgical order and reconcile differing factions. So, taken in context, Paul is not so much speaking about the role of women as he is speaking about liturgical order and about ending the chaos and confusion that reigned at Corinthian liturgical assemblies.

How do we interpret this passage for today? It is our responsibility as individuals within a faith tradition to interpret what this passage is saying to us today. Paul was speaking to a culture in which the role of women was profoundly different than it is in most cultures and societies today. His comments on women are the result of the culture in which he was writing. Today, we must ask what the proper liturgical roles are when we gather to celebrate Eucharist, what our present-day understanding of the equality and dignity of women is, and how the words of St. Paul can inspire us to celebrate liturgy with proper respect for its rubrics, roles, and order.

Interpretation Tools: Forms of Criticism

It is through the process of interpretation that the word of God continues to speak to people throughout the ages. The Bible was written at a time when most people were farmers or at least intimately familiar with rural life and lived under monarchic rule. When the biblical authors recorded their experiences of God's saving presence in their lives, they did not have a society of cellular phones, Internet-wired personal computers, and laser technology. For that reason, it is up to us to interpret the word of God as it applies to our contemporary situation. Despite the new world we live in, the central experiences of life remain unaltered. The word of God is timeless. We need only to transport it from its original setting and language to our contemporary situation. In order to do this, Scripture scholars offer us some very helpful tools for interpretation called forms of criticism. Let's take a brief look at some.

Historical Criticism This form of criticism attempts to ascertain as accurately as possible what the author's original intent was. Historical criticism looks closely at what was happening at the time, what the people of the time were experiencing, and the audience for whom the author was writing. Today, archeology plays an important role in learning as much as we can about the place and times of the Scripture passage in question. Another aspect of the historical approach is the attempt to determine who the author actually was. We know today that it was common practice in biblical times to credit a literary work to someone who may not have actually taken pen to paper. Today, we consider that fraud. Recall, however, that the Bible was recorded in a time when most people were illiterate. Most forms of literature were passed along orally for decades if not centuries before they were written down. As with any oral tradition, the stories take on the flavor of those passing them along. Since we believe that the Bible is the inspired word of God, we are saying that God inspired this entire process. In the end, as long as a piece of literature was said to have been from the tradition of an individual, it was deemed proper to add that person's name to the title of the book. In other words, when we say that something is by the prophet Isaiah, we are saying that this is indeed the message he conveyed as it was passed down orally for a given period before a scribe or school of scribes collected it, sorted it, edited it, recorded it, and credited it to his name. Once again, this does not take away from the validity of the Bible but reveals how God works through a very human process to shape the word into flesh. The better we understand this whole process, the closer we can come to the original intent of the work before we attempt to apply it to our own lives.

Textual Criticism When discussing Scripture, we will sometimes hear people say, "If we go back to the *original* text . . ." It sounds good. All we need to do is go back to the original text and see exactly what was written, translate it as closely as possible into English, and we'll know exactly what the text says. There's only one problem. We have no original texts. We do not have any of the psalms written in David's own handwriting on parchment. We have none of Paul's letters on the original stationery. All we have are early manuscripts . . . which are the earliest known *copies* of all the works of the Bible. When Scripture scholars "go back to the original text" then, they are going back to the earliest available copies. Textual criticism attempts to look at these early manuscripts, many of which contain inconsistencies among the different copies, and try to determine what they said in their original language so that the best interpretation can be made when translation is attempted.

Form Criticism With Paul's letter to the Corinthians, we talked about how important it is to know what type of literature you are reading. Form criticism attempts to determine precisely what type of literature we are dealing with, how that form of literature was understood in its time, and how we are to understand it today. Scripture scholar Dianne Bergant, C.S.A., uses an effective example in her classes at the Catholic Theological Union in Chicago to illustrate how different forms of literature are appropriate for different occasions. She refers to the experience of someone's death. We encounter many forms of literature that are associated with someone dying.

- a death certificate

- a last will and testament

- an obituary

- a eulogy

- stories

- a homily

All of these forms of literature have a unique purpose and a proper place when one says good-bye to a loved one. Some are legal documents. Some are informal anecdotes. Some are ritual expressions. We know how to sort these out and put them in their proper place; we know how to interpret them. Form criticism attempts to do the same. It is a way of sorting out what we are reading in the Bible and determining how to best interpret it given its literary form.

Source Criticism In today's literal and legalistic society, it is not only proper but also necessary for authors to indicate where they may have gotten an idea from. To use someone else's idea without giving proper credit is called plagiarism. In biblical times, this was not the case. It was common practice for one author to use other sources and edit, delete, incorporate, or expand upon them. Source criticism attempts to determine what previous sources an author may have had at his fingertips and how that source may have influenced the piece we are reading. Here's an example that works a bit like a word problem or a brain teaser: The Gospel of Matthew has more than 600 verses in it that appear in Mark's Gospel (which most scholars believe was written first). The Gospel of Luke, also written after Mark, contains more than 300 verses of Mark's Gospel. It seems clear that Matthew and Luke relied heavily upon Mark's Gospel to write their own. Strangely enough, however, Matthew and Luke have 240 verses in common that are *not* from Mark. Matthew and Luke were not written at the same time and in the same place or by the same author. How can they share 240 verses in common that cannot be traced to another earlier known Gospel? This mystery suggests to Scripture scholars that both Matthew and Luke had a source other than Mark upon which they relied to write their Gospels. Unfortunately, we do not know what this source was. Scripture scholars refer to this mysterious source simply as Q, the first letter of the German word *quelle* that means "source." Source criticism, then, attempts to look at the sources available to biblical authors and how these may have influenced later versions.

Redaction Criticism Take a look at the end of Mark's Gospel. Note that it has four endings. The story seems to end at Mk 16:8 when the women leave the tomb in great fear and say nothing to anyone. Next, we encounter something called the "Longer Ending," from Mk 16:9–20, which includes Jesus appearing to the disciples and ascending to heaven. Following this, we encounter something called the "Shorter Ending," which captures the essence of the longer ending in just a couple of sentences. Finally, we come upon something called the "Freer Logion," which may be in a footnote. This ending attempts to explain why the disciples were so hesitant to believe that Jesus had risen. If you read your footnotes and commentaries about these passages, you will learn that various early copies of Mark's Gospel end differently. These various endings appear to be attempts by "editors" to provide a more "satisfying" ending than Mark originally did in 16:8. Redaction criticism attempts to discover what portions of Scripture may have been altered or affected by later editors and why. These "alterations" should not be viewed suspiciously, nor should they in any way taint our understanding of the validity of the Scripture we are reading. Rather, they provide for us a window into the minds of people who were attempting to do just what we are doing: discover a way of making God's word "fit" into our lives. Their interpretation serves to inspire us to interpret the Bible for our own experience.

All of these forms of biblical criticism are not meant to strip the Bible of its power and mystery but open it up to us. We ourselves may not have conducted the actual scholarly studies and criticisms, but we should use the discoveries made by Scripture scholars to open our eyes to the richness of God's word and enhance our understanding of the Bible.

Where to Begin: A Recommended Reading List

Now that you've chosen your translation of the Bible and you're equipped with the knowledge and skills needed to read, study, and interpret the Scriptures, you may be wondering one more thing: where do I begin? If the Bible is indeed a library, then allow me to act as reference librarian for a moment and recommend some starting points.

THE OLD TESTAMENT

The first twenty chapters of the book of Exodus The Exodus story is the centerpiece of the entire Old Testament—the "defining moment" of the people of Israel, you might say. Besides, you can't go wrong with all of the drama and theatrics of burning bushes, deadly plagues, and parting seas.

The book of Psalms The Bible is intended to deepen our faith and our prayer life. What better place to begin than with an entire book of prayers? The Psalms will provide you with easy reading and profound inspiration for every mood and occasion.

The book of Proverbs If you are looking for wisdom, this is a good place to start. Reading Proverbs is like sitting down with your grandparents to get all of the profound insights they have collected through their years of experience. Many people begin and/or end their day with a passage from Proverbs.

THE NEW TESTAMENT

The Acts of the Apostles Acts is a good place to start because it is the story that most closely resembles our own experience—followers of Jesus struggling to preach the gospel after his ascension into heaven.

The Gospel of Mark If you want to get into the Gospels right away, begin with Mark. Mark's Gospel is the shortest and easiest to read. His "just the facts" approach allows you to cover the whole gospel story in just a few hours, something that is highly recommended.

The Letter of Paul to the Philippians Sit back and imagine that Paul is writing to you personally. This letter is inspirational and contains one of the most powerful and well-known Christian passages: Phil 2:5–11.

Tips for Reading and Praying the Bible

Typically, when you read a book, you just pick it up and jump right in. Reading the Bible is different. In essence, we do not *read* the Bible; we *pray* the Bible. Once you know what passage you are going to read (keep it short; don't try to take on too much), follow these simple steps:

1. Set a prayerful mood of quiet.

2. Pray to the Holy Spirit to open up your mind and heart to the word of God.

3. Read the passage once slowly. Look over any footnotes and commentary that will assist your understanding of the passage.

4. Go back and read the passage again, this time more slowly and prayerfully. If the passage describes a story or event, use your imagination to place yourself within the scene as a participant. Pause at phrases, words, or images that speak to you and allow them to resonate. Whereas your first read-through is for the head, this one is for the heart.

5. Be quiet. Let the word of God continue to echo in your heart, mind, and soul.

6. Pray in your own words thanking God for the word and asking for the grace you need to apply (interpret) it to your life.

This Is *My* Story

The refrain to the wonderful Christian hymn "Blessed Assurance" shouts, "This is my story." We should recall this refrain every time we pick up the Bible. Certainly, the Bible is full of stories about people who lived several thousand years ago in a land far, far away from most of us. Ultimately, however, these Bible stories are somehow the story of your life and my life. The reason these Bible stories are considered sacred and inspired is because throughout the ages, they have been seen as the stories that capture and express the experience of salvation for all people for all time. In other words, the Bible is about living now and forever—it is a living word!

As we read and pray the Bible, the ultimate act of interpretation is when we ask the question "How is this *my* story?" Unless we take this step, the Bible will remain something impersonal and remote. When we ask this question, we open up a whole new relationship in our lives. Now God is no longer just speaking to Moses, Abraham and Sarah, Jeremiah, Jonah, Peter, Zacchaeus, the woman at the well, Martha and Mary, and Paul. When we read the Bible—Paul's letters, Jesus' words to the apostles—we are hearing God speaking to us.

How do we make this happen? How do we make the Bible stories our own? We need to follow two simple steps:

1. First and foremost, we must ask what the text is actually saying and to whom it was originally addressed. Before applying the Bible to our own lives, it can be beneficial to understand the lives of the people who are involved in the story.

2. Second, once we have made an effort to understand the original intent of the author and the experience of the original audience, we must ask the simple and basic question "How is this story about me?"

When we do this, we realize that

- The Exodus event was not just about the journey of the people of Israel from slavery in Egypt to freedom in the Promised Land; it is the story of our own personal journey from the slavery of sin to the freedom we find in the place where we encounter God.

- The story of Jonah and the large fish is not just about a cowardly man turned prophet; it is the story of what happens to us whenever we try to run from the will of God—we find that God cannot be outrun.

- The stories of Jesus healing the blind, deaf, paralyzed, and unclean are not just tales of wonder from long ago; they are stories of how Jesus has the power to heal us when we cannot see, when our ears are closed, when we are paralyzed by fear, greed, or anger, and when we are stained by sin. The song "Amazing Grace" personalizes the experience by proclaiming, "I once was lost, but now am found, was blind but now I see."

- The story of Jesus appearing to the two disciples on the road to Emmaus is no longer just a mysterious story of two disciples who could not recognize Jesus; it becomes the story of how we seem to be unable to recognize the risen Christ in our midst until we listen to his word and break bread. In fact, this story contains a clue as to how we must insert ourselves into Scripture stories. Only one of the two disciples in the story is named: Cleopas. The other disciple remains unnamed. The author of this story seems to have done this on purpose in order to entice each one of us to insert ourselves into the story. *We* are the other disciple. *We* are often directionless. *We* have experienced pain and loss. *We* are unable to recognize the presence of Jesus even though he walks with us. It is through the reading and study of Scripture that we, like the two disciples on the road to Emmaus, develop a desire to gather around the table and break bread. When we do this, our eyes are opened and we recognize the presence of the risen Lord in our midst.

- In brief, the story of the woman at the well is the story of how we thirst. The story of the man born blind is the story of how we need to see with Jesus' eyes. The story of the raising of Lazarus is the story of how each of us is dead, wrapped up, buried, and in need of being called forth to new life. The story of the passion, death, and resurrection of Jesus is the story of how we come to be born again only by dying to our old selves. The story of Pentecost is the story of how we are gifted and sent forth by the Spirit to proclaim this Good News to others.

Now Is the Acceptable Time

During one of my God's Library presentations to a group of thirty-five to forty Catholic young adults, one participant admitted that she had only recently begun to learn about the Bible by attending Scripture study. She was excited about the new knowledge and nourishment that she was receiving. I asked her if she was attending this Scripture study at a Catholic church or a Protestant church. She turned red and sheepishly admitted that she was attending a Protestant Bible study. Not wanting to discourage her in any way or proliferate any form of anti-Protestant suspicion, I affirmed her zeal. I commented that while I would prefer that she attend a Catholic Bible study, if none were being offered, it was good that she was being nourished by the word of God from our Protestant brothers and sisters. Before I could move on, another participant strongly objected, not out of any distrust of Protestants but out of a sense of shame that no Catholic churches in the area were offering Bible study. He said, "If there are no Bible studies in any of the area Catholic churches, then, by God, we had better start one . . . now!" During the break, I observed as several participants surrounded the pastor eagerly offering to help set up a Bible study program for the parish. (See the appendix, p. 97, for suggestions on how to do this.)

I couldn't agree more with the young man's comments. The time has come for Catholics to take ownership of the Bible. To loosely quote St. Paul in his second letter to the Corinthians (6:2): "NOW is the acceptable time!" As St. Jerome once said, ✶ "Ignorance of the Scriptures is ignorance of Christ!" (Dei Verbum, #25). The Second Vatican Council stated firmly that "access to sacred Scripture ought to be open wide to the Christian faithful" (Dei Verbum, #22). The time has come for us Catholics to embrace, with enthusiastic zeal and profound openness, the gift of God's word given to us in holy Scripture. When it comes to our approach to the Bible, we should heed the words of Deuteronomy: "Take to heart these words which I enjoin on you today. Drill them into your children. Speak of them at home and abroad, whether you are busy or at rest. Bind them at your wrist as a sign and let them be as a pendant on your forehead. Write them on the doorposts of your houses and on your gates" (Dt. 6:6–9). Or to put it in a form more familiar to Catholics: (as we sign our forehead, lips, and breast before the Gospel each week at Mass): "May the Word of God be in our minds, on our lips, and in our hearts."

OPEN HOUSE AT GOD'S LIBRARY: YOU'RE INVITED!

God's Library is open twenty-four hours a day, seven days a week, 365 days a year (366 during leap years). Your borrowing privileges are unlimited: any book for any occasion. No limit on books per customer. No overdue penalties. No need to renew your borrowing privileges—they never run out.

Plan on taking a field trip to God's Library soon . . . and bring a friend!

QUESTIONS FOR REFLECTION AND DISCUSSION

- What does it mean to interpret the Bible? What do we need in order to safeguard against interpreting the Bible recklessly?

- What are some of the different types of literature you are familiar with in the Bible?

- What does it mean that every Bible story is somehow your story?

- How might your relationship to the Bible change as a result of this book?

How to Begin a Bible Program in Your Parish

The most important resources for beginning a Bible program in your parish are, first, people who desire to grow closer to God and, second, copies of the Bible! With these two resources serving as the foundation, your parish can begin a Bible program using a variety of resources available from many fine Catholic publishers.

Generally, there are three approaches to engaging people with the Bible. The first approach is **Bible discussion.** In this model, the goal is to give people a concentrated exposure to the scriptural texts, supported by solid scholarship, with the intention of inviting a personal response and practical application of the Scriptures to one's life. A popular example of this is Six Weeks with the Bible (Loyola Press). Bible discussion programs such as Six Weeks with the Bible are arranged in short, flexible installments that can fit easily into a parish Advent or Lenten program. At the same time, the flexibility allows for groups to stretch their discussion of a book or theme beyond the suggested time frame, depending on the needs of the group.

The second approach is **Bible study.** In this model, the goal is to deepen one's understanding of the Scripture text. Two examples of this approach are Little Rock Scripture Study (Diocese of Little Rock and the Liturgical Press) and the Denver Catholic Biblical School (Diocese of Denver). Bible study programs are like a Bible course. They are typically longer than a Bible discussion program, require homework, call for a greater commitment of participation, and need more skilled facilitation.

The third approach is **lectionary based.** In this model, participants enter into Scripture through the readings used at Sunday Mass throughout the liturgical year. A lectionary-based approach combines elements of both application and study with the additional goal of enhancing one's worship experience. A popular example of this is Celebrating the Lectionary (Resource Publications), which invites participants to study and reflect on the Sunday Scripture readings throughout the liturgical year.

Whatever model you select, here are some basic steps to follow in getting your program off the ground.

- Gather a core group of 3–4 people to meet with someone on the pastoral staff of the parish to propose a Bible program. Together, identify what it is that parishioners are looking for, and explore some of the Bible programs that are available from Catholic publishers. Select a model (Bible discussion, Bible study, lectionary based) that you feel meets the needs of parishioners. Likewise, identify and agree on some ground rules, such as the degree of participation and self-revelation that will be encouraged, how people will listen to one another, and how participants will maintain confidentiality.

- Together with someone from the pastoral staff, spend some time training two or three parishioners in the skill of facilitating. The facilitator is *not* a Scripture scholar or Bible expert; he or she is someone who is able, or can learn how to, move the process or discussion along in an orderly and effective manner.

- Survey parishioners to determine the most suitable day, time, and place for the program and coordinate logistics with the parish staff. If possible, offer the program at two different times and offer child care so that parents of young children can participate as well.

- Publicize well, not just in the parish bulletin. Request the opportunity to offer a two-minute invitation from the pulpit after communion at all the Sunday Masses, and follow up with an information table at the back of the church or in the parish center over coffee and cake.

The format of the gatherings should be simple enough so that the constant presence of parish staff personnel is not required. Lack of staff presence is no reason for Catholics not to engage in a Bible program. Programs such as Six Weeks with the Bible, Little Rock Scripture Study, the Denver Catholic Biblical School, and Celebrating the Lectionary provide guidance and background in their materials so that group leadership can focus on facilitating and not necessarily on Scripture scholarship. While most Bible study and discussion programs suggest a time format to follow, here is a generalized suggested format.

- Gather over refreshments for fifteen minutes. Be sure to select a setting that is comfortable and hospitable . . . avoid classroom atmospheres.

- The facilitator should welcome all participants and ensure that everyone has a Bible. Arrange to have on hand a number of Bibles of the same translation for those who do not have one. Again, the New American Bible is the one used in the U.S. Catholic lectionary.

- The facilitator should invite participants to locate the Bible passage(s) that will be the focus of the gathering. For example, in a lectionary-based program, the facilitator would indicate which Sunday of the liturgical year is upcoming and which readings will be proclaimed at Mass. Participants should locate the readings in their Bible with the assistance of the facilitator and other participants. This exercise is an important part of the study. Unless we begin to discover where these readings are in the Bible, we will continue to suffer from bibliaphobia. Avoid reading Scripture passages that are reprinted in other resources such as missalettes and workbooks . . . let's get those Bibles out and start using them.

- Light a candle and put on some reflective music. Spend three to five minutes in quiet preparation to read/pray the Scripture. You may also wish to invite all to stand and join hands in a circle and invite participants to offer out loud the prayers or petitions they bring with them. The only thing that Catholics sometimes fear more than reading the Bible is the notion of praying out loud with others. This format should encourage Catholics to become more comfortable with both.

- Often, programs will offer several general nonthreatening questions to begin discussion and lead participants to reflect on their own life experience before moving into Scripture. Generally, spend ten to fifteen minutes on this discussion.

- Invite one of the participants to slowly and prayerfully read the identified Scripture passage(s) while all follow along in their Bibles. If the passage is long, consider inviting participants to take turns reading sections. Pause in silence for a minute or two and then invite another participant or participants to read it again.

- Use your selected resources to provide background, commentary, and discussion questions based on the selected Scripture passage(s). Spend some time engaging participants in discussion using the resources you've chosen. You may also wish to ask a pastoral staff member or qualified parishioner to do a brief presentation on the background or commentary. Consider audio- or videotaping the minilecture for future use. Programs such as Little Rock Scripture Study offer the option of purchasing audio/videotaped lectures.

- During discussion, the facilitator should be sure to invite participants to offer insights and comments they have on the Scripture passage(s) and especially ways to apply insights from Scripture to daily living. Invite any questions that participants may have. Write down questions that cannot be answered by anyone present and designate someone to research the answer with a pastoral staff member or with assistance from the diocesan office.

- The facilitator can once again invite all to stand and join hands, inviting all present to share aloud prayers of thanksgiving. A sung refrain that can be learned and led easily may be sung as a way of giving praise as well.

- Invite participants to remain for refreshments, and invite them back again for the next session. Identify the focus of the next session as well as any "homework" that participants should do in preparation.

- Be sure to continue ongoing publicity, especially inviting new parishioners and the newly initiated. Avoid the temptation to become a clique. If the size of the group is becoming too large to allow for sharing and discussion, have a plan in place to break up into smaller groups led by additional trained facilitators.

- Note: Pastors and pastoral staffs are stretched thin with numerous responsibilities. The key to any Bible program format is to train parishioners to facilitate these gatherings so that they do not rely upon the presence of a staff member at all times. Such an approach allows staff members to attend occasionally or drop in regularly. Facilitator training programs are available from a variety of publishers to teach the skills of leading discussion, prayer, and handling difficult people and situations. Contact your diocesan catechetical office for assistance.

Finally, another thought to consider is the question of whether the proposed Bible program needs to be a parish program at all. Four or five couples can easily get together and do a Bible discussion without the guidance of the parish staff. With parish staffs stretched thin by the demands of their ministry, Catholics can take the initiative to pursue a deeper understanding of God's word on their own, using the quality materials provided by Catholic publishers.

Conducting a God's Library Workshop for Young People (Middle and High School Students)

This workshop can be accomplished in ninety minutes and requires one adult for every twelve to fifteen children. It may also be adapted for adults and young adults. The workshop requires that all participants have the same version of the Bible on hand so that page numbers can be used to locate passages quickly. It also requires that each participant have a set of the God's Library Bookmarks (see page 123) and a pair of scissors.

Goal: To build participants' familiarity and comfort with the structure of the Bible and to increase the ease with which participants locate books, chapters, verses, and famous stories/figures in the Bible.

Learning Outcomes: Participants will learn to quickly locate biblical books, chapters, and verses using the table of contents. Likewise, participants will learn to quickly identify the location of famous stories and figures by using the God's Library Bookmarks.

Action Plan:

1. Be sure all participants have the same version of the Bible, preferably the New American Bible.

2. Begin by introducing the notion of how important the Bible is to us as Christians and how we are going to

learn more about the Bible in this session. Ask how many have heard of the following stories (raise hands):

David and Goliath

Noah's ark

Jonah and the Large Fish

Jesus in the Garden of Gethsemane

3. Next, tell participants that you will offer a prize ($1 or $5, etc.) to the first person who can find one of these stories in the Bible in 60 seconds or less. Use a stopwatch (and a whistle) and give 60 seconds for each of the four stories listed above, one at a time (without adult assistance). Most likely, no one will be able to do so. (If you believe your audience is more astute than this, be sure to allow only 30–45 seconds lest you go broke!)

Point out how unfortunate it is that we know about these stories but we don't know how to find them in the Bible. Explain that we will be working on that in this workshop.

Next, tell participants to have their Bible ready. Write the following biblical citations on the board (be sure to use abbreviations):

Ez 12:6–8

Jb 2:3–11

1Thes 5:2–4

Again, allow participants 30–60 seconds to locate these passages (again, without adult assistance). Most will be unable to do so in the time allotted. Point out once again how unfortunate it is that we seem to be unable to identify Bible passages by their abbreviations. Ask if anyone can say out loud what the above abbreviations stand for.

4. Explain that if the Bible is so important to us, then we are going to need to learn how to find things in it more quickly and with more confidence. Explain that the Bible is not really a book but God's Library.

5. Explain that when you go to a library, you need to use the catalogue and the book-numbering system to locate the book you want to read. Point out how God's Library, the Bible, has a "catalogue," too, namely, the table of contents. Have all participants open their Bible to the table of contents section at the beginning. Adult supervisors should assist children here. Point out the alphabetical index, the abbreviations page, and other highlights of the table of contents in your version of the Bible.

6. Using the table of contents, invite participants to tell you what page the following books begin on:
    Deuteronomy
    Judges
    Esther
    Luke

Next, using the abbreviation table, ask participants to identify which book you are referring to when you write on the board:

Hb
Na
Ti

7. Using the board, point out how book, chapter, and verse are used in biblical citation:

Title of Book (abbreviated) Chapter:Verse(s)

Invite several participants to go to the board with their Bible open to the abbreviation table and write out in biblical citation the following passages as you say them:

Ecclesiastes, chapter nine, verses one to eight (Answer: Eccl 9:1–8)

Second Letter of Paul to Timothy, chapter two, verses four to six (2Tim 2:4–6)

(Select more, if you wish, depending on the size of your crowd, how quickly they are catching on, and how much time you have left.)

Once again, Scripture citation may be handled differently than what I've shown above, depending on which Bible you are using. While most Bibles use the system I've described, don't be surprised to find that some Bibles use a period or a comma instead of a colon to indicate the difference between chapter and verse. For example, the Scripture citation for the Gospel of John, chapter three, verse sixteen may appear in any of the following ways, depending upon which Bible you are using: Jn 3:16; Jn 3,16; or Jn 3.16.

Be sure everyone is "on the same page" with your approach to Scripture citation before you move on.

8. Now, explain how to find famous stories and passages when we don't know what book, chapter, and verse they are in. Use the concept of God's Library again and draw a diagram on a chalkboard (see diagram from page 14 in chapter 2). Imagine a building divided into two parts: Old Testament and New Testament. Ask how we differentiate between these two. (Answer: The Old Testament has stories about the people of Israel before Jesus; the New Testament has stories about Jesus and the Christian church.)

   Invite all participants to locate the place in the Bible where the Old Testament ends and the New Testament begins. Show how much larger the Old Testament is than the New. Ask participants what section they should be in if they are going to look for a story about Jesus.

9. Explain that in addition to breaking down the Bible into two large sections, we are now going to break it down into eight smaller sections, four in each testament. Distribute to each participant a set of God's Library bookmarks (see page 123) and a pair of scissors. (You may wish to have the bookmarks cut out ahead of time to avoid the use of scissors and to reduce the time spent cutting)

10. Beginning with the Old Testament, identify the four sections: Pentateuch, History, Wisdom, Prophets.

Have participants cut out and place one bookmark at a time, beginning with Pentateuch. Explain what can be found in this section by using the information provided on the bookmark. Have participants find the first and last page of each section, list the books included in this section, and insert the bookmark at the end of the section. For example, the Pentateuch bookmark goes on the last page of Deuteronomy. Invite the participants to hold up the Pentateuch section alone (take the section between the thumb and index finger) to observe its length. Using the bookmark, point out what stories/ people can be found in this section. Invite participants to locate a few. Do the same for each of the four sections of the Old Testament.

11. Do the same with each of the four sections of the New Testament: Gospels, Acts, Letters, Revelation. Point out that while Acts and Revelation are individual books and not really "sections," it is easier to separate them this way. Continue cutting out and inserting bookmarks one section at a time as you give a brief overview of what can be found in each section. Encourage participants to locate some stories as you talk about them. Spend extra time pointing out the Gospels section. Ask participants to hold up the section from Matthew through John: emphasize that if you want to find a Jesus story, this is where to look. Remember that all of the information you need is on the bookmarks.

12. Once all the bookmarks have been inserted, continue drilling participants as time allows, locating famous stories and figures in the Bible from the information provided on the bookmarks. Award prizes (candy, etc.) for just being in the right section (i.e., Pentateuch, Letters, etc.)

13. Encourage participants to continue quizzing themselves at home until they can remove the bookmarks as they would training wheels—when they are able to locate famous stories and figures within just a few minutes by knowing which section to look for. Encourage participants to show their parents, friends, pastor, etc. how they have learned to find their way around the Bible with such ease and familiarity.

Annotated Bibliography for Catholic Scripture Study

Church Teaching

Divino Afflante Spiritu (Pius XII, 1943), "By the Spirit's Divine Inspiration" (on Scripture). In this papal encyclical, often called "the charter of Catholic biblical studies," Pope Pius XII urges Catholic biblical scholars to read the Bible according to the literary genre in which each book was written. All papal documents can be found on the Vatican Web site: www.vatican.va.

"Dogmatic Constitution on Divine Revelation" in *Vatican Council II: Conciliar and Post-Conciliar Documents*. Rev. ed. General editor, Austin Flannery. Dublin: Dominican Publications, 1992. The "Dogmatic Constitution on Divine Revelation," although one of the briefest of the documents issued by the Second Vatican Council, is, at the same time, one of the most important, since it asserts that Scripture and sacred Tradition form the foundation of the Catholic faith. Inspiring.

Besides the Vatican II "Dogmatic Constitution on Divine Revelation," several other important documents relating to the Bible have come from the Pontifical Biblical Commission.

"On the Historical Truth of the Gospels" (1964) may be found in the appendix to Joseph A. Fitzmyer's *A Christological Catechism: New Testament Answers*. Rev. ed. New York: Paulist Press, 1991, 153–64. This document is the first official church statement espousing the value of form criticism (see *God's Library*, page 87). In it, the Biblical Commission explains that the Gospels as we have them today are the result of three stages: Jesus' words as heard by the disciples, the disciples' oral proclamation, and the work of the evangelists.

"Scripture and Christology" (1984) in Joseph A. Fitzmyer's book of the same name, *Scripture and Christology*. New York: Paulist Press, 1986, 3–53. In this document, the Biblical Commission outlines the relationship between biblical interpretation and theology.

The Interpretation of the Bible in the Church ([1993] in *Origins* 23, no. 29 [January 6, 1994]: 498–524) was also printed as a booklet by St. Paul Books and Media, Boston. This document reviews the key features of various methods of biblical criticism and outlines the characteristics of authentic Catholic interpretation and the interpretation of the Bible in the church's life. Very practical and clear.

Bibles

The Catholic Study Bible. New York: Oxford University Press, 1990. Besides the text and notes of the New American Bible with revised New Testament and Psalms, this volume features more than 600 pages of rich introductory material written by the best of contemporary American Catholic biblical scholars. It includes maps, glossary, lectionary listings, and more. Valuable for the educated general reader.

The Catholic Bible: Personal Study Edition. New York: Oxford University Press, 1995. The New American Bible accompanied by simplified versions of the introductory material of the Catholic Study Bible listed above. Good for beginners.

The New Jerusalem Bible. New York: Doubleday, 1985. Excellent contemporary British translation famous for its informative study notes, further enhanced for the second edition. The Old Testament notes surpass those of the current New American Bible. However, note that the less expensive Reader's Edition of the NJB does not contain study notes.

Reference Works

The Collegeville Bible Commentary. 2 vols. Collegeville, MN: Liturgical Press, 1992. Passage by passage explanations of each book of the Bible; good for beginners.

The Collegeville Pastoral Dictionary of Biblical Theology. General editor, Carroll Stuhlmueller. Collegeville, MN: Liturgical Press, 1996. Rewarding short studies of key ideas and themes. Each article studies its subject in the context of Scripture, but is made twice as valuable by including a section on the subject as it has been treated in the pastoral and liturgical tradition.

Dictionary of the Bible. John L. McKenzie. New York: Touchstone, 1995. Originally published in 1965, this reprint edition is a remarkable, very inexpensive work with short articles on thousands of biblical topics. A steal!

The HarperCollins Bible Dictionary. General editor, Paul J. Achtemeier. San Francisco: HarperCollins, 1996. Short, scholarly articles on a full range of biblical subjects.

Collegeville Bible Commentary Series, Collegeville, MN: Liturgical Press, 1998. Extensive commentary on books of Scripture from a Catholic perspective by international Scripture scholars, with welcome attention to the history of interpretation by the church fathers. Valuable.

The New Jerome Biblical Commentary. Raymond Brown, Joseph Fitzmyer, and Roland Murphy, eds. Englewood Cliffs, NJ: Prentice Hall, 1990. The preeminent work of Catholic biblical scholarship. For advanced students.

The New World Dictionary-Concordance to the New American Bible. New York: World Publishing, 1990. More of a dictionary than a concordance, but great for beginners.

Secondary Works

These authors are some of the most well-respected contemporary Catholic theologians. Here are some of their more groundbreaking works.

Alter, Robert. *The Art of Biblical Narrative.* New York: Basic Books, 1981. This and the next volume represent some of the best of the new literary study of Scripture.

———. *The Art of Biblical Poetry.* New York: Basic Books, 1985. Also very revealing.

Boadt, Lawrence. *Reading the Old Testament: An Introduction*. New York: Paulist Press, 1984. A basic work, very helpful.

Brown, Raymond E. *The Critical Meaning of the Bible*. New York: Paulist Press, 1981. Rewarding essays on the Catholic Church's engagement with critical Scripture scholarship by one of the leading Catholic biblical scholars of our time.

———. *Responses to 101 Questions on the Bible*. New York: Paulist Press, 1984. Question-and-answer-style discussion treating common questions. Brown never dodges an issue.

———. *Biblical Exegesis and Church Doctrine*. New York: Paulist Press, 1985. Short essays exploring traditional Catholic positions such as the virginal conception of Jesus in the light of modern scholarship.

———. *Introduction to the New Testament*. New York: Doubleday, 1997. Will be the standard advanced introduction to the New Testament for the next generation.

Brueggemann, Walter. *The Bible Makes Sense*. Atlanta: John Knox Press, 1977. Creative and stimulating invitation to read Scripture.

Cavalletti, Sofia. *History's Golden Thread: The History of Salvation*. Chicago: Catechesis of the Good Shepherd Publications, 1999. Well-crafted, richly suggestive tracing of typological relations in the Scriptures. Welcome vision of the Old and New Testaments as one word of God.

Chilson, Richard. *Full Christianity: A Catholic Response to Fundamental Questions*. New York: Paulist, 1985. A well-written book for the general reader, it uses a question-and-answer format to show the differences between the Catholic and fundamentalist visions of Christianity.

Days of the Lord: The Liturgical Year. 7 vols. Collegeville, MN: Liturgical Press, 1991. Solid reflections on passages from the lectionary. Translated from French.

Fitzmyer, Joseph A. *A Christological Catechism: New Testament Answers.* Rev. ed. New York: Paulist Press, 1991. Questions and answers on who Jesus was according to the Bible from a Catholic perspective. Includes the text of the Pontifical Biblical Commission's 1964 "On the Historical Truth of the Gospels."

Grant, Robert M., with David Tracy. *A Short History of the Interpretation of the Bible.* 2nd ed. Philadelphia: Fortress Press, 1984. Fascinating panorama of the perspectives and uses to which Scripture has been put. Tracy's section gives a philosophical orientation to contemporary issues in biblical hermeneutics.

Harrington, Daniel J., S.J. *Interpreting the New Testament: A Practical Guide.* Collegeville, MN: Liturgical Press, 1990. First volume of the New Testament commentary series gives background to the series and reviews modern methods of New Testament study.

———. *Interpreting the Old Testament: A Practical Guide.* Collegeville, MN: Liturgical Press, 1991. First volume of the Old Testament commentary series gives background to the series and reviews modern methods of Old Testament study.

Hestenes, Roberta. *Using the Bible in Groups.* Philadelphia: Westminster Press, 1983. Basics of group Bible studies. Protestant perspective.

———. *The Writings of the New Testament.* Rev. ed. Minneapolis: Augsburg/Fortress, 1998. Well-written introduction with acute attention to each book's final literary and theological shape. For advanced students.

Kodell, Jerome. *The Catholic Bible Study Handbook*. Ann Arbor, MI: Servant Books, 1985. Readable book touching on development, background, and approaches to the Bible.

Martin, George. *Reading Scripture as the Word of God*. 4th ed. Ann Arbor, MI: Servant Publications, 1998. Knowledgeable, wise help for approaching a disciplined practice of reading the Scriptures by a gentle guide who discovered the path for himself. Excellent.

Perkins, Pheme. *Reading the New Testament: An Introduction*. Rev. ed. New York: Paulist Press, 1988. Basic introduction to content and themes of the New Testament; strong on historical background.

Books of the Bible and Their Abbreviations

List of Books and Abbreviations in the Order in Which They Appear in Your Bible

OLD TESTAMENT

Genesis	Gn	1 Chronicles	1Chr
Exodus	Ex	2 Chronicles	2Chr
Leviticus	Lv	Ezra	Ezr
Numbers	Nm	Nehemiah	Neh
Deuteronomy	Dt	Tobit	Tb
Joshua	Jo	Judith	Jdt
Judges	Jgs	Esther	Est
Ruth	Ru	1 Maccabees	1Mc
1 Samuel	1Sm	2 Maccabees	2Mc
2 Samuel	2Sm	Job	Jb
1 Kings	1Kgs	Psalms	Ps
2 Kings	2Kgs	Proverbs	Prv

Ecclesiastes	Eccl	Luke	Lk
Song of Songs	Sg	John	Jn
Wisdom	Ws	Acts of the Apostles	Acts
Sirach	Sir	Romans	Rom
Isaiah	Is	1 Corinthians	1Cor
Jeremiah	Jer	2 Corinthians	1Cor
Lamentations	Lam	Galatians	Gal
Baruch	Bar	Ephesians	Eph
Ezekiel	Ez	Philippians	Phil
Daniel	Dn	Colossians	Col
Hosea	Hos	1 Thessalonians	1Thes
Joel	Jl	2 Thessalonians	2Thes
Amos	Am	1 Timothy	1Tm
Obadiah	Ob	2 Timothy	2Tm
Jonah	Jon	Titus	Ti
Micah	Mi	Philemon	Phlm
Nahum	Na	Hebrews	Heb
Habakkuk	Hb	James	Jas
Zephaniah	Zep	1 Peter	1Pt
Haggai	Hg	2 Peter	2Pt
Zechariah	Zec	1 John	1Jn
Malachi	Mal	2 John	2Jn
		3 John	3Jn

NEW TESTAMENT

Matthew	Mt	Jude	Jude
Mark	Mk	Revelation	Rv

Alphabetical List of Books and Abbreviations

OLD TESTAMENT

Amos	Am	1 Kings	1Kgs
Baruch	Bar	2 Kings	2Kgs
1 Chronicles	1Chr	Lamentations	Lam
2 Chronicles	2Chr	Leviticus	Lv
Daniel	Dn	1 Maccabees	1Mc
Deuteronomy	Dt	2 Maccabees	2Mc
Ecclesiastes	Eccl	Malachi	Mal
Esther	Est	Micah	Mi
Exodus	Ex	Nahum	Na
Ezekiel	Ez	Nehemiah	Neh
Ezra	Ezr	Numbers	Nm
Genesis	Gn	Obadiah	Ob
Habakkuk	Hb	Proverbs	Prv
Haggai	Hg	Psalms	Ps
Hosea	Hos	Ruth	Ru
Isaiah	Is	1 Samuel	1Sm
Jeremiah	Jer	2 Samuel	2Sm
Job	Jb	Sirach	Sir
Joel	Jl	Song of Songs	Sg
Jonah	Jon	Tobit	Tb
Joshua	Jo	Wisdom	Ws
Judges	Jgs	Zechariah	Zec
Judith	Jdt	Zephaniah	Zep

NEW TESTAMENT

Acts of the Apostles	Acts	Mark	Mk
Colossians	Col	Matthew	Mt
1 Corinthians	1Cor	1 Peter	1Pt
2 Corinthians	2Cor	2 Peter	2Pt
Ephesians	Eph	Philemon	Phlm
Galatians	Gal	Philippians	Phil
Hebrews	Heb	Revelation	Rv
James	Jas	Romans	Rom
John (Gospel)	Jn	1 Thessalonians	1Thes
1 John	1Jn	2 Thessalonians	2Thes
2 John	2Jn	1 Timothy	1Tm
3 John	3Jn	2 Timothy	2Tm
Jude	Jude	Titus	Ti
Luke	Lk		

Bibliography

Bergant, Dianne. *Introduction to the Bible*. Collegeville Bible Commentary: Old Testament. Vol. 1. Collegeville, MN: Liturgical Press, 1985.

Brown, Raymond E., Joseph A. Fitzmeyer, and Roland E. Murphy, eds. *The Jerome Biblical Commentary*. Englewood Cliffs, NJ: Prentice Hall, 1968.

The Catholic Study Bible: New American Bible. New York: Oxford University Press, 1990.

Charpentier, Etienne. *How to Read the Old Testament*. John Bowden, trans. New York: Crossroad, 1982.

The Complete Parallel Bible, Containing the Old and New Testaments with the Apocryphal/Deuterocanonical Books: New Revised Standard Version, Revised English Bible, New American Bible, New Jerusalem Bible. New York: Oxford University Press, 1993.

"Dei Verbum, Dogmatic Constitution on Divine Revelation," 18 Nov. 1965, in *Vatican Council II: The Conciliar and Post Conciliar Documents*. Austin Flannery, O.P., General Editor. Collegeville, MN: Liturgical Press, 1975.

Ludwig, Robert A. *Reconstructing Catholicism: For a New Generation*. New York: Crossroad, 1995.

Pontifical Biblical Commission. "The Interpretation of the Bible in the Church," in *Origins* 23, no. 29 (January 6, 1994).

Rolheiser, Ronald. *Against an Infinite Horizon: The Finger of God in Our Everyday Lives*. Rev. ed. New York: Crossroad, 2001.

Witherington, Ben. *Conflict and Community in Corinth: A Socio-Rhetorical Commentary on 1 and 2 Corinthians*. Grand Rapids, MI: Wm. B. Eerdmans, 1995.

PENTATEUCH

Genesis through Deuteronomy

Place this bookmark on the last page of the book of Deuteronomy. Welcome to the section called the "Pentateuch" or "Torah," meaning the five books of the Law. This section captures the beginnings of the relationship between God and the people of Israel with the central focus being of the event . . . the experience of being led from slavery to freedom. Here are some of the highlights:

- the creation stories
- Adam and Eve
- Cain and Abel
- Noah's ark
- the tower of Babel

Section highlights continue on reverse

HISTORY

Joshua through 2 Maccabees

Place this bookmark on the last page of 2 Maccabees. You've now entered the History section of God's Library—the section that records the story of the people of Israel who, under various leaders (judges and kings), fought to establish and keep the Promised Land. Here are the highlights:

- Joshua (crossing the Jordan, the walls of Jericho)
- Samson and Delilah
- Ruth and Naomi
- Samuel (request for a king)
- King Saul
- David and Goliath; King David
- Solomon (the temple, queen of Sheba)

Section highlights continue on reverse

WISDOM

Job through Sirach

Place this bookmark at the end of the book of Sirach. You're now ready to explore the Wisdom section of the Bible. While the Bible contains wisdom throughout, this section collects the wisdom of the people of Israel over thousands of years of wandering the desert, living in the Promised Land, worshipping in the temple, and struggling through exile. Among the many anecdotes, sayings, prayers, poems, and songs, here are some highlights:

- Job's suffering
- 150 Psalms for all occasions

Section highlights continue on reverse

PROPHETS

Isaiah through Malachi

Place this at the end of the book of Malachi and welcome to the last section of the Old Testament—the book of the Prophets. The prophets were not concerned with foretelling the future as much as with calling the people of Israel back to their past fidelity to God, lest they face doom. Likewise, they held out hope for the future when the people of Israel found themselves in dire consequences in exile. This hope was the notion of a messiah and an everlasting kingdom. Yet even these assurances of a future are accompanied by a call for a return to the fidelity of the past. Here are some highlights:

See reverse for section highlights

PENTATEUCH

Genesis through Deuteronomy

- Sodom and Gomorrah
- Abraham and Sarah
- Isaac and Rebekah
- Jacob and Esau
- Joseph (the coat of many colors)
- Moses (in the reeds, the burning bush, the ten plagues, the crossing of the Red Sea, the Passover, the Ten Commandments, the Ark of the Covenant, the journey through the desert, the death of Moses)
- the twelve tribes of Israel
- the laws, traditions, and feasts of Israel

HISTORY

Joshua through 2nd Maccabees

- Elijah and Elisha
- many kings, battles, and genealogies
- division of the kingdom
- exile and return
- Judith and Esther

WISDOM

Job through Sirach

- hundreds of proverbs
- wise sayings, including "Vanity of vanities, all things are vanity!" and "There is a time for everything" and "A faithful friend is a sturdy shelter" and more
- a romantic love song (Song of Songs, or Song of Solomon)
- thousands more sayings about wisdom, prudence, good health, wealth, holiness, family, friends, misery, death, and even table etiquette

PROPHETS

Isaiah through Malachi

The major (meaning lengthier) prophets

- Isaiah (Immanuel, "the people who walked in darkness have seen a great light," "comfort my people," etc.)
- Jeremiah (call of Jeremiah, exile and return)
- Ezekiel (the dry bones)

The minor (meaning briefer) prophets, including

- Daniel (the lions' den, Shadrach, Meshach, and Abednego)
- Hosea (the unfaithful wife)
- Joel (the Day of the Lord)
- Amos (the call to justice)
- Jonah (swallowed by a large fish)

Place this bookmark at the end of the Gospel of John and prepare to enter the part of God's Library where we walk with Jesus! The Gospels contain the stories that are most sacred to our Christian faith and heritage: the life, teachings, miracles, passion, death, and resurrection of Jesus of Nazareth. Here are some highlights:

- the birth of Jesus (the Magi, the shepherds, etc.)
- the Holy Family (Mary and Joseph)
- the finding of Jesus in the temple
- the temptation in the desert and the baptism of Jesus
- the Beatitudes and the Our Father

Section highlights continue on reverse

This section of the Bible is easy because it is just one book–the Acts of the Apostles. Place your bookmark at the end of this book and relive the experience of the early Christian community. In many ways, the book of Acts is a sequel to the Gospel of Luke because both were written by the same author. Here are some highlights of the Acts:

- Jesus' ascension
- the descent of the Holy Spirit on Pentecost
- descriptions of the communal life of the early church
- Stephen's martyrdom
- Philip and the Ethiopian

Section highlights continue on reverse

Place this bookmark at the end of the letter of Jude. Welcome to the communications of the early church, before there were e-mail, phones, and faxes. Of the twenty-one letters, a little more than half are attributed to Paul. All of the letters are addressed to communities of Christians and to the leaders of these communities and were designed to teach, admonish, encourage, correct, and update the various churches. Here are some highlights:

The letters of Paul (e.g., Romans, 1 and 2 Corinthians, Galatians, and Ephesians) feature theology, teachings, and exhortations concerning:

Section highlights continue on reverse

Place your last bookmark at the end of the book of Revelation and you've reached the end of the Bible! As you enter the book of Revelation, be aware that it is one of the most misunderstood books of the Bible. Many falsely use this book to predict the end of the world. Written in apocalyptic language, the book of Revelation uses many symbols and figurative language to describe the eternal struggle between good and evil. Despite all of the frightening imagery, the uplifting conclusion of this book is that good has and always will prevail. Here are the highlights:

See reverse for section highlights

GOSPELS

Matthew, Mark, Luke, and John

- parables
- the Golden Rule and the great commandment
- numerous miracles and healings
- the Last Supper, Eucharist, and the washing of the feet
- the agony in the garden
- Peter's denial and Judas's betrayal
- the way of the cross and the Crucifixion
- the Resurrection and appearances
- dozens of fascinating characters: Zacchaeus, Mary Magdalene, Nicodemus, the Samaritan woman, Martha and Mary, etc.
- powerful images such as the Bread of Life, the Light of the World, the Way, the Truth, and the Life

ACTS OF THE APOSTLES

- Saul's conversion and baptism
- the missionary work of Peter, Saul (Paul), Barnabas, and others
- miracles performed through Peter and Paul
- Paul's travels, imprisonment, trials, shipwreck, and arrival in Rome

LETTERS

Also called Epistles

Romans through Jude

- grace
- justification by faith
- the Law
- the Eucharist
- the metaphor of the Body
- variety and unity of gifts
- ministry
- suffering
- Christ and his cross
- Christian conduct

James: faith and good works, and anointing of the sick

1 Peter: be prepared to explain your hope

1 John: "Beloved, let us love one another . . ."

REVELATION

- visions of and messages to the seven churches
- the scroll and the Lamb
- the 144,000 saved
- the seven trumpets
- the woman and the dragon
- the King of kings
- the thousand-year reign
- the new heaven and new earth
- the new Jerusalem
- "Come, Lord Jesus!"